M000308393

SEATTLE'S BEST
DIVE BARS

SEATTLE'S BEST DIVE BARS

DRINKING AND DIVING IN THE EMERALD CITY

MIKE SEELY

Brooklyn, New York

Copyright © 2009 by Mike Seely
Photos copyright © 2009 by Cary Melton
All rights reserved.
Printed in the USA
10 9 8 7 6 5 4 3 2 1

No part of this book may be used or reproduced in any manner without written permission of the publisher. Please direct inquires to:

Gamble Guides is an imprint of
Ig Publishing
178 Clinton Avenue
Brooklyn, NY 11205
www.igpub.com

Seattle's best dive bars : drinking and diving in the Emerald City /
Mike Seely.
        p. cm.
 ISBN 978-0-9815040-1-8
 1. Bars (Drinking establishments)--Washington (State)--Seattle--
Guidebooks. 2.
Seattle (Wash.)--Guidebooks. I. Title.
 TX950.57.W22S44 2009
 647.95797--dc22
                            2009006103

Seattle's Best Dive Bars
(arranged by neighborhood)

Acknowledgements

For my family, Joel, Duke & Pat, Sweet Baby Swain, Aistrope, Tommy Rotten, everyone at *Seattle Weekly*, and the Olympia Brewery tour guide who convinced me at age eight that drinking beer was the coolest thing in the world.

All photos by Cary Melton except where otherwise indicated.

Waterwheel Lounge *(Scott Manley)*

Preamble

I was nursing a Rainier at Al's, a classic watering hole in Wallingford, when a wise patron imparted the following words of wisdom. "Martinis are like tits," he announced. "One's not enough and three's too many."

Hilarious adage? Yes. True? No; at least not as far as the drinking establishments in this book are concerned. While one's certainly not enough, three martinis—or any kind of drink, for that matter—are just the tip of the nipple at Seattle's best dive bars, where every day's a Friday.

Some dives have vomit-caked toilet seats in the bathroom; others have cracked vinyl booths in the barroom. Some have nicotine-stained murals dating back to the Depression; others have drink prices that seemingly haven't wavered since then. Some are the most welcoming places you could ever hope to encounter; at others, if you're not homeless or an ex-con (or con-in-waiting), people will look at you as though the jukebox should stop immediately. Still others split the difference: Given the right about of lubrication, two previously unacquainted patrons will be just as likely to embrace at the end of the night as beat the snot out of one another. Usually, which way this scenario tilts depends on whether political or musical preferences get brought up. Around Seattle, them's fightin' words.

But really, no collection of characteristics can be melded to truly define what makes a bar a dive. And for every barkeep who considers being lumped into this misunderstood genre a slur, there'll be two others who consider such branding a gesture of affinity. With the overwhelming majority of bars in this book, the term "dive" is bestowed with a salty spoonful of love. By and large, the places chronicled herein are the most unique, preservation-worthy bars in a city where watering holes of this ilk are swiftly disappearing. What they have in common aren't so much attributes, but a state of mind—you just know one when you see one. And if I had to encapsulate precisely what this moment of recognition felt like, I'd do it through the eyes of an old soldier named Wayne, whom I encountered in a downtown Everett bar in the fall of 2008.

With a few hours to kill before a Saturday night rock show down the street, I sidled up to the bar at the Doghouse on Colby Avenue. In the cooler were cans of Old Milwaukee and Schmidt (if there's a telltale sign you're in a dive bar, Schmidt's it). Behind me was seated a stoic gentleman, slowly nursing a beer and talking to nobody. The small TVs were tuned to nothing particularly important. Playing pool was a middle-aged Latino fellow who confessed to having no recollection of how he got home from the bar the prior night. He also said his head hurt, which couldn't have surprised anyone.

Bellied up in the far corner was a beefy, mustachioed tow-truck driver, downing vodka shots and bitching loudly about how retarded his customers were. As I ordered my second Schmidt, a weary fellow named Wayne sat down to my immediate left. He said he'd just returned home from a long trip. I asked him where he'd been. "Cabo," he responded. I said, "Well, that doesn't sound too rough." He looked at me like I'd just killed the Pope, and said, "Whaddya mean?"

Turns out I'd heard wrong: Wayne was in Kabul, having just completed his next-to-last 18-month tour of Iraq. At the age of 53, he was due to ship back out in a few days. Feeling like shit on a shoe, I insisted upon buying Wayne a drink. He took me up and ordered a shot of Southern Comfort. I ordered one too.

Wayne is from Alaska, but lives on his boat near downtown Everett. (In his divorce, she got the house, he took the boat.)

Before heading back to the Middle East, Wayne remarked that the one thing he most wanted to do while home was go kayaking, chilly weather notwithstanding. It's hard to imagine an activity further removed from engaging in combat in the smoldering desert, where Wayne recently lost one of his best friends to a roadside bomb.

After ordering another round of SoCo, Wayne remarked that the reason he'd come to the Doghouse that Saturday afternoon was because he knew it would be exactly the way he remembered it the last time he was here some four years ago. He'd come to the bar because it was reliable, a reminder of home that he could look forward to visiting again once his final tour ended. I told him when that day came I'd meet him there, and buy us another round of shots.

Dive Ratings

All dives are rated on a scale of one to five mugs of Rainier, with five being the diviest.

🍺 One toothless old man at the bar.

🍺🍺 One toothless old man under the bar.

🍺🍺🍺 One toothless old man behind the bar.

🍺🍺🍺🍺 Leave your valuables at home.

🍺🍺🍺🍺🍺 Drink and be merry, for tonight you shall die.

NORTHWEST SEATTLE

GREENWOOD
BALLARD
FREMONT
MAGNOLIA

Sloop Tavern

2830 NW Market St.
Phone: 206-782-3330

If you wanted to distill Seattle's drinkers into an extremely pure weight class system, you might say there are but two types: sailors and everyone else. It's not so much that sailors can outdrink the average desk jockey—although they usually can—it's their day-to-day resilience that separates them from the herd. What for most people would spell a surefire head-ringer of a hangover with the potential to incapacitate for at least a day is just another night at the bar for a sailor. For the sailor, drinking and socializing at the nearest onshore watering hole every night is as much a ritual as breakfast. And sometimes, it is breakfast.

The sailors of Shilshole Bay Marina, many of whom live aboard their vessels year-round, have it pretty good. About a mile from where they're moored, near the Ballard Locks, is a remodeled government-run liquor store that, tellingly, is the state's most lucrative, as well as two sit-down drinking establishments, the Lock Spot and the Sloop Tavern. Both serve very good fish and chips and both are occasionally graced by the presence of a *Deadliest Catch* cast member, but that's where the similarities end. And given that the Lockspot serves hard booze and the Sloop has only beer and wine (Washington State's booze regulations could easily be confused with Utah's, they're so draconian), they complement one another rather nicely.

A spacious working-class tavern with lots of arcade games, the Sloop sells 34-ounce "Slooper-size" mugs of Rainier beer for $3.75. (Rainier, once brewed south of downtown, is now brewed out-of-state by Pabst Brewing Co.) Among its more loyal customers are sailors and men who work in the maritime industry on either side of the Puget Sound Ship Canal, as much of the Alaskan fishing fleet docks along this channel during off months.

The Sloop is so intertwined with Ballard's seafaring culture that it actually doubles as a yacht club. The tavern sponsors a 22-race schedule, highlighted by an early-May round-trip booze bender designed to counteract highfalutin Seattle Yacht Club's opening day. In this vein, it's tough to imagine any of the sailors at the Sloop actually christening their sloops, unless it's with a forty of High Life, the champagne of beers.

Dive Bar Rating: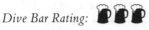

Mike's Chili Parlor

By its very location at the foot of the Ballard Bridge, Mike's Chili Parlor represents one of the city's more visceral snapshots of old versus new Seattle. Near Mike's, where factories and warehouses used to be are now a Christian hipster megachurch, a modern monstrosity of a building housing one of Bill Gates' charities, a humungous Fred Meyer, and a gargantuan mixed-use retail complex that includes a Trader Joe's.

Then there's Mike's, a low-slung brick building that's occupied the corner of 15th Ave NW and Ballard Way since 1939. The business actually dates to well before then: Founder Mike Semandiris began selling chili from a cart to maritime and industrial workers along the nearby Ship Canal in the '20s before putting a roof over his parlor's head.

Mike's used to just serve beer along its signature chili, which despite its tendency to make diners' asses explode like intestinal piñatas, is enough of a local icon that it was recently featured on the Food Network. The steak fries are great, too, especially with chili drizzled over them (everything here should be eaten with chili drizzled over it). And ignore the fact that grilled cheese sandwiches are listed at $53.75 a pop on the menu board. That's false advertising.

Thanks to a recent relaxation in what sort of establishments can and can't serve hard booze, Mike's now has higher octane behind the bar. Whatever part of me hates this transformation is quickly silenced once young Mike—the original Mike was his great-granddad—pours me some Ouzo the way Ouzo was meant to be poured: in a small rocks glass with an ice cube, for sipping. Mike's also offers schooners with its pitchers. It's just easier to drink beer out of a schooner than a pint glass. I'm not sure why this is, but it is.

The regulars at Mike's have not changed with the neighborhood. While on occasion, groups of younger patrons will occupy a table, the customers are generally as salty as the sea from whence they toil, just like back in the day. Hopefully Mike's won't go away when this type of guy goes away. Or, better yet, hopefully these guys will never go away.

Dive Bar Rating: 🍺🍺🍺

Jonathan Tuttle

Ballard Smoke Shop

5443 Ballard Ave. NW
Phone: 206-784-6611

As recently as the mid-1990s, there weren't a lot of good reasons to visit Ballard Avenue—but being a drunk was definitely one of them. At the northern end of the street were three watering holes—the Smoke Shop, Vasa Grill, and the Sunset Tavern—where customers could start drinking at 6 a.m. and not have to quit until 20 hours later, provided their legs didn't give out first. Then they'd get (or stay) up and do it all again, a vicious, 80-proof cycle if there ever was one.

Today, Ballard Avenue, with its cutesy boutiques, high-end pet stores, and swank eateries, is fully gentrified. The Vasa Grill is now the German-themed People's Pub, and the Sunset has been made over into a popular hard-rock venue. Only the Smoke Shop remains intact, and while it welcomes the inevitable interloping hipster into its doors, it's still the same as it ever was—except for the "smoke" part.

Like California and New York before it, Washington State began enforcing an indoor smoking ban in 2005. While the sky-is-falling prognoses favored by the owners of many nicotine-stained places of drink turned out to be untrue in a general sense (after an initial dip, bar revenues quickly returned to and even exceeded pre-ban levels at most establishments), there was a feeling—even among non-smokers such as myself—that certain places should have been exempted from the ban outright, that not being exposed to second-hand smoke somehow sullied the souls of certain places.

The Smoke Shop is one of those places. Like a lot of establishments whose regulars tend to get a little tipsier than your average bar, the Smoke Shop keeps its female bartenders in heavy rotation, as even the drunkest of boys won't be boys if the person serving them isn't a boy. What's more, Smoke Shop bartenders are so used to deciphering slurred, run-on sentences that they're like seeing-eye dogs for drunks, or master translators for an inebriated U.N. floor debate.

For the truly obliterated, there's the Smoke Shop's soup, which bartenders will spoon up unsolicited if they feel the need to nurture a drinker who looks as though he's turned the corner down one of whiskey's darker alleys back to a sunnier patch. This simple, ingenious act of human kindness is commemorated on t-shirts that read, "I Got Souped at the Smoke Shop." Unlike the soup, the shirts will set you back some.

Dive Bar Rating: 🍺🍺🍺🍺

Golden City

5518 20th Ave. NW
Phone: 206-782-6809

Seattle has a large Asian-American population, and thus features more than its fair share of Asian restaurants. Many of these restaurants have lounge areas that are at least as prominent as the restaurants themselves, and most of these lounges fit rather neatly into what most people would consider a dive. Judging from these establishments, utility reigns supreme in Asian culinary culture. The very existence of dim-sum carts backs this notion up, as dim-sum is the ultimate fast food experience.

I could devote half this book to lounges at Chinese restaurants, but that would be like fishing with dynamite. Golden City, however, really breaks the mold. Let's start with the mural that appears to your left as you enter the lounge area. There are whites and blacks getting off a steamboat, and the black people in this mural look to be subservient to the nattily-dressed whites. At best, this is a Civil War-era mural; at worst, it's a maritime slave mural. Almost assuredly, it's not *intended* to offend anyone; the mural's probably just been there for eternity, and no one's seen much cause to remodel. Remodeling a Chinese lounge would be sort of blasphemous, after all, as drinks hardly get stiffer based on how few stains there are on the carpet. In fact, the opposite's usually true.

Another Golden City surprise: the jukebox features a lot of southern rock and live Grateful Dead albums. In the age of Internet jukeboxes, which offer you the world in the most sterile of packages, simply finding a traditional jukebox anywhere is refreshing. Finding one whose tunes seem to have been curated with genuine TLC is downright mind-blowing, especially in places where you'd least expect it.

While there seems to be a deep familiarity between bartenders and regulars seated at Golden City's bar, there's inevitably a corner table where something secretive will be transpiring. Maybe the embers of an extramarital affair are being stoked, or maybe the sort of information that exists behind the veil of attorney-client privilege is being transmitted. That's the thing about bars like this: Either everybody knows your name or nobody does. There's extreme value in either dynamic.

Dive Bar Rating: 🍺🍺🍺🍺🍺

STIFFEST DRINKS

MOON TEMPLE

GIM WAH

GOLDEN CITY

BALLARD SMOKE SHOP

SEVEN SEAS

THE RIMROCK

THE BARANOF

F.O.E #2141

5216 20th Ave. NW
Phone: 206-783-7791

Eagles Clubs aren't bald yet, but they're threatening to be. Like so many fraternal organizations of the animal kingdom—Elks, Moose, Lions—the Eagles have had difficulty attracting a new generation to its flock. The fact that I, at 34, am one of the youngest members of the Fraternal Order of Eagles' Aerie 2141, commonly known as the Salmon Bay Eagles, should speak volumes here.

There are Eagles Clubs all over the world, but the first was Seattle's Aerie #1, which was founded in 1898. Originally located downtown, Aerie #1 subsequently moved to its present home in Georgetown. Ballard, meanwhile, used to be home to two Eagles Clubs: one Aerie 2141 near Ballard Ave., the other the Ballard Eagles, which were located near the intersection of 24th and Market. The Ballard Eagles' (Aerie 172) former home was cavernous; compared to it, the Salmon Bay affiliate was something of a red-headed stepchild.

But in the year 2000, the rich got greedy, as the Ballard Eagles entered into what they thought was a sweetheart deal with a developer who wanted to transform their one-story property into an office building. On the first floor of the building was to have been spiffy new digs for the Ballard Eagles. But the developer ended up getting thrown in the pokey for embezzling $87,000 from the organization, and the Ballard Eagles were left without a home.

In the wake of its brethren, Aerie 2141 plugs along. The interior of the building is a throwback to an era when bars were known as saloons, and the men's room contains a tricky entry step that even teetotalers should be mindful of. There is an elevated level containing a stage, which plays host to live blues, karaoke, and a cover band that can pull off "Whiter Shade of Pale" with aplomb. Drinks and meals are served at cut-rate prices, and female members are not full-fledged members, but belong to an "auxiliary." Looked at squarely, that could be construed as rather sexist. Looked at from a fiscally prudent angle, women's annual dues are half those of men. From this perspective, every night is ladies' night. See how easy that was?

The Salmon Bay Eagles—or any Eagles Club, for that matter—can best be described as a country club for people who would never be admitted into an actual country club. That's not intended as a slur; remember: I'm one of them, not the guy in the ascot and blazer. Besides, I'd rather drink with people who've spent life on the outside looking in.

Dive Bar Rating: 🍺🍺🍺🍺

Hattie's Hat

5231 Ballard Ave. NW
Phone: 206-784-0175

If you want to find a bar whose history most closely mirrors that of its street—and perhaps the neighborhood at large—you could do far worse than to walk into Hattie's Hat, a vintage lounge-diner hybrid that rivals the Smoke Shop for longest tenure on Ballard Avenue.

Hattie's is located on the same block as the Tractor Tavern, a well-respected Americana music venue that's owned by Dan Cowan, who also has a stake in the Hat. Closer still is King's Hardware, so named because it's housed in what used to be part of the Ballard Hardware empire. King's is owned by Linda Derschang, who's built her own empire of rustic-looking hipster haunts that are designed to ape the manly, carnivorous saloons of the Mountain West.

The arrival of one of one of Derschang's bars was viewed by longtime Ballardites as the surest of signs that the neighborhood had officially jumped the shark (Derschang has achieved most of her success on Capitol Hill). But while King's arrival was accepted with an air of inevitability, the same can't be said for when Cowan and his partners installed a fish tank in the rear dining area of the Hat.

For a place with cream corn and chicken fried chicken on its menu, the floor-to-ceiling tank was jarringly out of character. But in the front of the house, renovations were so subtle as to be unnoticeable. Booths were expanded to accommodate more patrons, but the wall-length mural, side service counter, and historic bar remained undisturbed.

On balance, the remodel left Hattie's a bit shinier without sacrificing much character. If you knew nothing of Hattie's history—up until the '90s, it was the sort of place where booze-fueled fights would spill out onto the sidewalk in the middle of the day—you might take it for a faux-dive, the sort of place Derschang would build from scratch. But within Hattie's walls is enough true grit to ensure its continued inclusion in the hang-dog realm. Like much of Ballard Avenue, it's found a way to age gracefully without forgetting where it came from.

Dive Bar Rating:

Jonathan Tuttle 25

The Waterwheel Lounge

7034 15th Avenue
Phone: 206-784-5701

The Waterwheel doesn't look like the sort of place that serves up quality home-style food—or any food at all, for that matter. It looks like the sort of place where you might get your head bludgeoned on the rim of a toilet by a hulking longshoreman named Ted who's been drinking boilermakers since sunrise.

Situated on the North Ballard urban hodgepodge of 15th Avenue Northwest, where tarot readers, strip joints, and classic brick and mortar businesses abound, the Waterwheel's look is pure roadhouse chic. It's essentially housed in a red doublewide, and its parking lot is gravel. Inside, there is one pool table, a handful of tiny round tables with high chairs, and a long, rectangular bar. The doors are often left open to let natural light creep in, which feels intrusive unless you're seated on the recently-opened deck, which sits no higher than the gravel lot itself. When that light does creep in, you realize that this bar might contain the most dust particles per square foot in the free world, or at least Ballard.

The bartender who typically works during the afternoon is a sweet, matronly woman named Susan. Sometimes she wears track pants and flip-flops to work. The crowd during these hours is almost exclusively male, and it's simply amazing the quality of all-American chow that emerges from this doublewide's kitchen—although if they're slammed, be prepared to wait awhile.

Every time I go to the Waterwheel, I half expect Gregg Allman to walk in. This seems like the sort of bar where an old road warrior would seem right at home, even if the track marks are fresher than he or his NA sponsor would like them to be. It's also the sort of bar where mixed drinks should be banned. A shot of tequila with a Busch back is more the Waterwheel's speed. After a few of those combos, the dust starts to clear.

Dive Bar Rating:

Viking Tavern

6404 24th Ave. NW
Phone: 206-784-3662

One of life's great mysteries is why more bars don't have urinals that go all the way to the floor. It's not like bathrooms will small urinals make use of the space beneath the bottom of the porcelain egg to store shit. Hence, while urinals that stretch to the ground may be bigger and longer, they're actually a more efficient use of space. Plus, when you're at a bar, your aim's more liable to be off, and the longer urinals allow for a greater margin of error.

Like the most accommodating of Scandinavian dive bars, the Viking has urinals that extend to the floor. Unlike most Scandinavian dive bars, it also serves great barbecue sandwiches, smoking its own brisket, pork, and ribs daily (they even smoke their potatoes here, and do so in what employees claim to be the state's smallest kitchen). Occasionally, there's Guinness mixed into the sauce; otherwise, it's comprised of Coca-Cola, brown sugar, and various spices. The Sloppy Joe is called a Sloppy Sven, and the homemade chili's quite good. But make no mistake: the Viking is still very much a drinking man's establishment. The fact that patrons are afforded the option of ingesting something tasty for their Rainier to wash down is just frost on the beard.

The Viking has been around since 1950 and is located next door to a standard issue barber shop, making it an easy source of nostalgia. This mood is enhanced by the narrow bar's vintage ceiling fans, stools, smooth wooden bar, and shuffleboard. Across the street is a bar called the Copper Gate, which boasts an exterior that screams shithole. Well, it used to be a shithole; and used to form quite the one-two punch of inebriation when paired with the Vike. But now, the Copper Gate is a sleek nouveau-Nordic haunt that serves high-minded food—only the façade looks tough. The Viking's having none of that hypocrisy.

Dive Bar Rating:

Ed's Kort Haus

6732 Greenwood Ave. N.
Phone: 206-782-3575

In many ways, Ed's Kort Haus is a quintessential Seattle dive. It's dark and spacious, with a pool table and horseshoe bar. It features an auxiliary station near the kitchen which seems to function more as a storage space for dusty rec-league trophies than as a beverage center. Televisions large and small are hanging from the ceiling, seemingly at random. The exterior is painted a hideous shade of green. Whereas workaday bars in other parts of the country might feature one or two domestic beers on tap, Ed's dutifully continues the Seattle dive bar tradition of carrying a ridiculous amount of microbrews on tap in addition to the obligatory Rainier and Bud.

But the Kort Haus has a few quirks that'll make the average Seattleite feel like an odd duck. For one, there are two arcade games devoted to buck hunting, a predilection said to be native to southern Illinois (having lived back that way for awhile, I can vouch for the accuracy of this statement). Then there's the dry-erase board situated above one of the arcade games. On it are the names of a dozen or so wild animals: alligator, antelope, black bear, buffalo, spicy buffalo, camel, caribou, elk, spicy elk, kangaroo, llama, ostrich, reindeer, venison, wild boar, and yak. This peculiar list comprises Ed's vast offering of exotic burgers. (Also listed are jackalope, unicorn, and elf, obviously the work of a wiseacre regular.)

Ed Warrington, a mercurial, mustachioed fellow who's owned the bar for 27 years and named it in his own honor, has his meat air-freighted in from all over the globe. He gets his buffalo from Wisconsin, his alligator and camel from Australia, and his antelope and venison from a 2.5-million-acre ranch in Texas. While the exotic burgers began as a one-off experiment, they now account for 30 percent of all the burgers Warrington sells and have become something of a local curiosity, as novice patrons can often be found ordering them with a shot and a chuckle.

The hunting games, the wild burgers that could easily be confused with a list of endangered species, the quip on the menu that reads "Proprietor not responsible for missing animals from Woodland Park Zoo" (the zoo's less than a mile down the road)—if this isn't the biggest inadvertent fuck-you to PETA of all time, then I don't know what is.

Dive Bar Rating: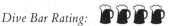

R. Oscar

Yen Wor Garden

8580 Greenwood Ave. N.
(2nd location in West Seattle)
Phone: 206-784-0455

Confidential to karaoke deejays everywhere: no one wants to hear you sing. This should be a simple rule for KJ's to follow, but it's not. Granted, when you think about what motivates deejays—vanity—their tendency to want to take their turn in the rotation becomes a bit more understandable, but not to the point of absolution.

If, for some reason, the KJ decides that it's unethical to get up and sing a ditty himself every few songs (early in the night or when the house is dead, mind you, this sort of behavior is completely justifiable), he may revert to a second, far more subtle method of control freakiness. Here's how the racket works: I'm at the bar by nine o'clock, when karaoke starts. For the first hour, I'm up to bat every sixth song or so, which grants me two or three reps. But then the place starts to fill up, and requests from new singers flood the KJ's booth. Never mind that when this flood begins, my request to sing "Footloose" is on deck, the megalomaniacal KJ will bump my request down the ladder until every last new singer has gotten his or her turn on stage.

These are the sort of KJ felonies that occur on a regular basis at the Greenwood Yen Wor. To make matters worse, the bartender's a coarse bitch, and not in a good way. The good kind of coarse bitch is one that requires you to know exactly what you want the moment she's ready to take your order. There was a coarse bitch like this who used to work at the Frontier Room back in that bar's previous, super-shabby life, and I absolutely adored her. Her demeanor all but kept the amateurs out. But the bartender at Yen Wor is the worst kind of coarse bitch, the kind that gets annoyed that she actually has to take your order in the first place. Answer me this: Isn't the whole point of having a bar to sell drinks? Flipping shit and putting up a brassy front is all good and well, but does it make any sense to sincerely and needlessly antagonize customers?

At the Greenwood Yen Wor, it apparently makes a ton of sense. All of these foibles don't seem to make a lick of difference; the Yen Wor is so conveniently located within Greenwood Avenue's underrated nightlife district that people flock here anyway. As for me, about the only good thing I can say about the place is the rear entrance is pretty cool; walking through various nooks and crannies en route to the lounge, it feels as though you're mimicking a poor man's version of the steady-cam shot in *Goodfellas*.

Dive Bar Rating:

KARAOKE DIVES

THE RICKSHAW
THE BARANOF
YEN WOR
OZZIE'S
SYLVIA'S LITTLE RED HEN
CHANGES
THE CRESENT
BUSH GARDEN

The Baranof

As Seattle has gotten cooler, in both its own eyes and those of the world, Seafair has gotten decidedly less cool. What was once a great festival of citywide pride is now dismissed as a cheesy relic of Seattle's former backwoods status. Well, it is cheesy. Anything centered on clowns, pirates, parades, and hydroplane racing is bound to be cheesy. But it's still pretty great—at least for the one day in late July when the Green-wood Parade takes place.

Many neighborhoods have Seafair parades, but few are looked upon as an excuse to take work off and drink all day. So it goes in Greenwood, a northwest Seattle neighborhood that has yet to turn as trendy as, say, Ballard. And on parade day, the fulcrum of the debauchery for neighbors and pirates alike is the Baranof. While this venerable restaurant-lounge does steady business throughout the year (their food is a lot better than you'd expect it to be), on parade day it's so crowded that people are climbing over one another to get to the bar. And they're all completely shitfaced.

The neat thing about the Seafair Pirates is that, in spite of their focus on entertaining children, they genuinely enjoy getting loaded. The Baranof is as good a place as any to do this. Given the shanty-like décor, low ceilings, and narrow corridor between bar and tables, the Baranof can feel like drinking beneath the deck of a ship at sea, which probably explains why the Pirates love it. Another explanation: The veteran cadre of female bartenders typically go temporarily deaf around the time you utter the "and seven" part of your "bourbon and seven" order, which results in more quench for your thirst.

There's a more spacious room with a stage that adjoins the bar. Here, they occasionally have karaoke, only it's that rare no-bullshit brand of karaoke where the deejay doesn't fancy himself a rock star (Jesus Christ, have *American Idol* and MySpace created an ever-increasing army of delusional vocalists). Instead, KJ duties are handled by a longtime regular named Gilligan, who simply calls singers up in sequence with virtually no editorial commentary. This is how it should be.

Dive Bar Rating: 🍺🍺🍺🍺🍺

Jonathan Tuttle

The Crosswalk

8556 Greenwood Ave. N.
Phone: 206-789-9691

The Crosswalk is called the Crosswalk because there's a crosswalk in front of the bar's front entrance. There's exactly zero nuance to the name, and very little subtlety to the bar either. This stark, musty space is plenty big, but rarely more than half-full. It's good for pull tabs and Sunday afternoon football-watching, and there are pennants and random sports paraphernalia spread haphazardly throughout the bar. It actually feels weird drinking at the Crosswalk after nightfall, as by then, most of the action has moved across the street to the Baranof, next door to the Yen Wor, or further north on Greenwood to the Rickshaw.

Like the Baranof, the Crosswalk has been around since downtown Greenwood was generally regarded as a working-class armpit. Unlike the Baranof, the Crosswalk has not caught fire with younger folks as the neighborhood has become more of a destination. But hey, there's something to be said for a bar whose energy peaks in the middle of the afternoon, when the underbelly of alcoholism is most nakedly exposed.

People who have the time to tie one on at noon on a Tuesday are either retired, have just gotten out of prison, have no job, are underemployed, or are self-employed, which, in many cases, is just a glossed-up term for unemployed or underemployed. All of these people are usually more interesting than the sort of person you're likely to come across at a popular after-work spot in a more upscale neighborhood, and they'll all make you feel a lot better about yourself. Sure, you might have passed out on your ex-fiancée's kitchen floor while her new boyfriend fucked her in the next room, but at least you don't have to pay alimony and submit to random drug tests. It's all about perspective, see.

Dive Bar Rating: 🍺🍺🍺🍺

Pacific Inn Pub

3501 Stone Way N.
Phone: 206-547-2967

Blocks removed geographically yet miles removed attitudinally from Fremont's meet market scene, the dinky Pacific Inn has long embodied the classic Northwest tavern: clean, small, and simply appointed, with a good jukebox, dynamic beer selection, and great fish and chips. While it's added a small deck and hard booze to its arsenal and the crowd is no longer dominated by bearded men in rubber coveralls, the Pac-Inn refuses to cave to the whims of a neighborhood and city drunk on San Franciscan aspirations.

I first visited the Pacific Inn in college on the advice of some upperclassmen, who described it as a tavern where "cool girls go." By "cool," they meant fiercely independent young women who wore jeans and very little makeup, and liked sports, beer, and the Stones. In other words, they meant my dream girl.

Now I know guys who like a dash of drama in their love life; they want a high-maintenance bitch who'd rather go to the gym than the bar after work and who takes two hours to prep for an evening out. This is the sort of woman who insists upon heated leather car seats and the Black Eyed Peas with Fergie, who carries hand sanitizer in her purse and a frown on her face should she ever find herself forced to enter a bar like the Pacific Inn.

Thankfully, you're far likelier to find this sort of filly down the street at the Triangle (not to be confused with the White Center or Pioneer Square bars of the same name) or Ballroom. And for the popped-collar and striped-shirt dweebs who loves 'em: Good luck chipping the foundation off your pillow in the morning, fellas, and thanks for leaving the brown-eyed women and red grenadine to me.

Dive Bar Rating: 🍺🍺🍺

Heads or Tails

With its cheap, throwback motels and vast swaths of archaic, for-get-me-now storefronts, it is no wonder Highway 99—once the main artery connecting the United States' entire West Coast—has devolved into Seattle's foremost thoroughfare of cheap and sleazy vice in the era of eight-lane interstates. It's not the sort of environment that lends itself easily to cozy neighborhood pubs, to put it mildly, and the rare drinking establishment that does emerge tends to reflect the transient nature of the strip.

Like the road it rests along, Heads or Tails is a bar without a cohesive aesthetic. In one corner, there are plush loveseats and a fireplace, and the pool table is so close to the front entrance that you're apt to get poked in the gut by a cue's backswing. Between the fireplace and felt are three or four tables, and then a random couch near the one-room bar's southern wall.

The crowd of a couple dozen is all male, save for the bartender and a black chick with a shiny shirt rubbing her ass against the crotch of an Ian Holm look-alike dressed in a sweater and a crisp pair of Dockers. It would be no reach to assume their relationship is that of client and service provid-er, but then the picture gets blurry, as two other dudes —one a soused guy in khaki chinos, the other a beady-eyed grease monkey—converse frequently enough with the pair to make it evident that they're a party of four, and probably not a party of four that will morph into a three-on-one at the Motor Inn across the street once someone sinks (or snorts) an eight ball.

After they finish playing, they duck outside for a smoke—along with what seems like half the bar, including the bartender. Again, this being Aurora, it would be easy to assume that wher-ever they've gone, they're up to no good. But old guys in khakis? It doesn't quite add up; and the grease monkey turns out to be a real prince to boot, complimenting my eyewear and welcoming me into "the four-eyed club," of which he's a member too.

Dive Bar Rating: 🍺🍺🍺🍺🍺

Gim Wah

3418 W. McGraw St.
Phone: 206-284-7000

The Gim Wah is the only dive bar—and one of the few bars, period—in the majestic Magnolia community, where, if you're fortunate enough to own property, you know you're drinking from one of Seattle's sweeter troughs of nectar. But on Magnolia's northeastern slope, down the hill from the sparkling hillside manors that overlook Puget Sound, is an anonymous, blue-collar apartment-land known as Interbay, the presence of which is probably responsible for the continued operation of the Gim Wah, even though the bar physically rests on the ritzier side of the tracks.

Legend has it that a Gim Wah regular once walked out of the bar and stumbled into the Mexican restaurant next door, where he sat down, ordered a beer, suffered a heart attack, and keeled over. So well known was this fellow's appetite for drink that the staff just assumed he'd passed out, and didn't bother to tap him on the shoulder for a full 20 minutes—at which point they realized he was dead.

The Gim Wah's front shudders are perpetually shut; if it's a sunny day outside, its customers will never know. It is a small, dark bar, with a Buddha statue in one corner, a neon Michelob sign, and another neon sign directly beneath it that says "Noddles"—which makes you think for a second that Michelob is best paired with a bowl of noodles. Who knows? Maybe it is.

The crowd at the Gim Wah is a congenial mix of retired bullshitters, dads looking for a quick break from domesticity, and otherwise lonely apartment dwellers. At happy hour, it has a Cheers-like feel, while later at night it's either very quiet or semi-filled with adventurous youngsters who live nearby. A mixed drink is rarely mixed—a token squirt of soda in a bourbon and soda is what you'll get instead. And cementing the bar's status as an uber-dive is the most repulsive-smelling men's room in the city; the olfactory sensation upon entry is tantamount to being waterboarded with urine instead of H2O.

Dive Bar Rating: 🍺🍺🍺🍺🍺

The Bit Saloon

4818 17th Ave. NW
Phone: 206-782-1680

Rule number one for being a cool dive bar: Don't advertise the fact that you're a dive bar. On the awning above its front entrance, the Bit Saloon anounces itself as "Ballard's quirkiest dive bar," which annoys me to the point where this otherwise deserving establishment almost got left out of this book—until a sticker on one of its bathroom walls made me reconsider such a snub.

The bathroom in question is unique in that it boasts only a metal, trough-style urinal and no stalls. Here, affixed to the wall above the sink is a small sticker that reads: "All employees must wash hands after taking a dump"—in a bathroom where it's impossible to take a dump. Okay, Bit, all is forgiven.

The Bit's tendency to plead for working-class credibility is hardly germane to the current management: At the start of the 21st Century, the Bit was owned by well-intentioned guy who overreached by proclaiming that the Bit was "the place for working folks." To make matters worse, the Bit's neon horse head makes it a sort of wannabe Buckaroo. On the other hand, the new owners have transformed the bar into a very respectable live music (mostly country or really hard rock) venue without sacrificing the lower-key comforts of the adjacent barroom. Rainier beer runs a very reasonable $7 per pitcher, and the door policy is canine-friendly.

But maybe the best thing about the bit is the crowd. At other Ballard bars, the blue-collar lifestyle is something that is fetishized by hipsters with degrees from Reed, Oberlin, and Brandeis —their boots are just too damn clean, their demeanor too staid. But with the Bit's sloppily jubilant clientele, one gets the feeling that these are young people who actually earn their keep through jobs that require elbow grease. Maybe this is the place for working folks after all.

Dive Bar Rating:

Wingmasters

If you don't believe in curses, consider the following true story. The University of Washington football team is getting throttled by the mighty USC Trojans a week after the Huskies' coach, Tyrone Willingham, announced he'd be stepping down at the end of what would turn out to be a winless season. At the bar is a large woman dressed in denim overalls with a gray ponytail down to her ass. She's double-fisting whiskey and beer and slurring her words as though she's developmentally disabled, which she just might be. As the Trojans run up the score, the woman reminds everyone in the bar, sometimes within an inch of a person's nose, that she's a huge Trojan fan —figuratively speaking, of course. As if that weren't enough, she goes on to claim that she actually went to Southern Cal (bullshit).

Noticing that she's inebriated to the point where her trips across the room to gloat begin to resemble more wobble than walk, I remark off-hand that I hope her booze-induced journey into a state of unconsciousness is predicated by a colossal spill at the bar. Sure enough, not five minutes pass before she attempts to sit in her stool, leading with her right arm. Only her elbow slips clumsily off the stool's brass back, sending her colossally fat ass straight to the floor. She's helped up by a couple guys, one of whom, the bartender, is laughing hysterically —at least in part at himself, on account of the fact that he's failed to scrub all the makeup off his face after a Halloween night spent in drag.

While the poultry-based delicacy touted in its moniker is more than serviceable, Wingmasters would be an unspectacular neighborhood dive were it not for its mozzarella sticks, which are closer in size to Jimi Hendrix's erect penis than the deep-fried twigs you'll find at most places. I made the mistake of touting the uniqueness of these cheesy boners in the *Seattle Weekly* one summer, and they've only grown in size since, to the point where it'd be more accurate to call them "blobs" than "sticks." But still, their boundless ambition is a sight to behold. *Dive Bar Rating:* 🍺🍺🍺

Goofy's

8519 15th Ave. NW
Phone: 206-783-5164

NORTHWEST * CROWN HILL

SEATTLE'S BEST DIVE BARS

The crowd at Goofy's could serve as central casting for a unique Seattle species: the north Seattle wigger (I wish there were a better term than this, really I do). This species has emerged in large part because: (a) there are very few black people in north Seattle, (b) black culture has long been perceived as edgy and cool in the eyes of upper middle-class whites, and (c) in adolescence, due in part to the lack of black classmates to keep their affectation in check, upper middle-class white males take it upon themselves to wig out and fill the void, artificially and idiotically.

When black people act like black people, it's cool—it's who they are, where they come from, what they're down with, what their parents had to endure. When white people try to act like black people, they come off as culturally oblivious, tone-deaf poseurs who fail to grasp the nuances from which the persona emerges. Fortunately, the north Seattle wigger usually comes to his senses and stops acting like someone he's not by the time he's of legal drinking age. But some are stamped for life, and they evidently like to drink at Goofy's, which takes on the feel of a Ballard or Ingraham High School reunion on some weekend nights. The ambiance is "1/3 ski cabin, 1/3 Uncle Tom's Cabin, and 1/3 Log Cabin Republican," says one Ingraham alum, and the food is strictly of the gut bomb variety.

In keeping with Goofy's tacky, glory days vibe, it's the sort of bar that moves you to buy platter after platter of kamikazes for a gaggle of fat chicks who've just finished the early stages of a bachelorette party at the male strip joint next door, go home with one of them, snap out of a blackout at about 5 in the morning, sprint out the door with one shoe on, and stumble back to your abandoned Volkswagen, which has had its tires knifed by a competing suitor from the night prior.

What's worse, you left your wallet on her nightstand.

Then again, this drink 'til you drop m.o. is part of Goofy's appeal. Furthermore, the Crown Hill bar occasionally serves as an unlikely venue for hard rock shows, and serves drinks befitting the hard rock lifestyle. And in a town where to rock out with your Hawk out is the only acceptable way to take in a pro football game, Goofy's serves as a refreshingly notorious hangout for Green Bay Packer fans on Sundays from September through January.

Dive Bar Rating: 🍺🍺🍺🍺

Van's 105 Tavern

602 N. 105th St.
Phone: 206-789-9005

For those unfamiliar with Seattle's greatest multi-directional thoroughfare, shortly after 15th passes 85th St., it becomes Holman Road. At Greenwood Ave. N., Holman morphs into N. 105th St. (further east, it becomes Northgate Way). On this road, equidistant from the Rickshaw to the west and Cyndy's House of Pancakes to the east, sits a diminutive watering hole called Van's 105 Tavern.

What's most striking about Van's is how bright it is inside, a beacon of light in a relatively hardscrabble North Seattle neighborhood. Rockabilly quietly plays on the jukebox and the Mariners replay on FSN is tuned in on the TV, which an aging war veteran named Art with a Marine Corps hat on watches intently while drinking a can of Schmidt.

Seated near Art is a much younger, larger fellow named Galen, who drinks beer straight from a mini-pitcher and feeds the female bartender a steady stream of good-natured guff. When another young lady enters the tavern, accompanied by a skinny, good-looking guy, Galen asks her if she's ever been married. She replies that she's had several husbands, but only one of them has been rich.

After finishing his beer, Art gets up and wobbles around a bit before heading to the men's room. When he comes back, he orders another Schmidt, which Galen pays for. The couple that's just entered asks to have the volume on the jukebox turned up a bit, but only if it's okay with Art. He says that the volume can be turned up slightly, so long as he can still hear the Mariner telecast.

Galen then launches into a balanced commentary the Reagan presidency, commending the Gipper for staring down the Russians during the Cold War, but skewering him for his decision to snub the air traffic controllers' union. Here, Galen goes so far as to finger this standoff as being responsible for "the death of the middle class," pointing out that to qualify as middle class in modern-day Seattle, one has to pull down a six-figure income.

Of this hardship, the novelist Tom Robbins remarks: "Nobody wants to be working class anymore. Even bohemians want to drink champagne nowadays. It's part of the gentrification that is reducing the soul of Seattle, and gentrification is tied to upward mobility."

Dive Bar Rating: 🍺🍺🍺

DON'T SERVE HARD LIQUOR

THE SLOOP

THE BUCKAROO

THE ALKI TAVERN

POGGIE TAVERN

THE RED ONION

STREAMLINE TAVERN

EASTLAKE ZOO

VAN'S 105 TAVERN

PIONEER SQUARE SALOON

The Buckaroo Tavern

4201 Fremont Ave. N.
Phone: 206-634-3161

A Fremont institution for over 70 years, the Buckaroo has thrived largely by standing firm against the winds of change. But in Seattle, declining to serve hard booze these days has become tantamount to refusing to use the Internet or get a cell phone.

"[The trend toward full liquor licenses] makes everybody think that everybody's going to jump on the bandwagon," says the Buckaroo's owner, Donna Morey, whose husband and business partner, Keith, passed away not too long ago. "Simply because I'm older, I probably will sell in the next 10 years. For the time being, we're holding out as a beer-and-wine tavern. That is our hope: that we can hold out at least until I'm no longer around. We've been a tavern for 70 years, so we're going to try to keep with our ordinary traditions we've always run on—wine and beer and good cheer."

There might come a point when holding fast to tradition will become perilous for Morey's bottom line, but it should be noted that the Buckaroo is no ordinary tavern. Rather, it's one of few bars where bohemians and bikers drink shoulder to shoulder without exchanging harsh words, and it'd undoubtedly be the first stop for the cast of *Easy Rider* if they were passing through town (the Blue Moon would be the second).

The Buckaroo's exterior resembles an Old West saloon, with neon figurines lighting up the night sky. The interior is all wobbly stools and wood, with no shortage of clever, crass etchings. There are very few tables, but a fair amount of solo seating lines the walls, and there's a shelf of metal pool lockers next to the bathrooms.

Cinematic fun fact: Jennifer Jason Leigh was shot drinking in the Buckaroo's back booth in the Seattle-based film *Georgia*, right before she took the stage and sucked the life out of a Van Morrison tune. Next to that back booth is a stack of

SEATTLE'S BEST DIVE BARS

keg shells and a Golden Tee arcade game. Most Golden Tee units are created equal, but not the Buckaroo's. The screen is slightly discolored and the greens are treacherously fast, like at Augusta National. If Dennis Hopper in his drunken prime were to play 18, it'd doubtless result in a busted machine.

Dive Bar Rating: 🍺🍺🍺🍺

The Four B's

4301 Leary Way NW
Phone: 206-782-9024

The Four B's—short for Ballard's Best Brew & Burgers—harkens back to a time, not too long ago (although virtually unfathomable to those under 30), when Ballard was a civic punch line. The stereotype had it that Ballard was an unsophisticated mix of fishermen, auto mechanics, elderly Scandinavians, and live-for-the-moment burners who kept listening to Poison long after grunge came and went. And according to *Almost Live*, Seattle's woebegone local equivalent to *SNL*, none of these Ballardites could properly operate a motor vehicle, sober or otherwise.

Ballard's come a long way since then. The Four B's hasn't, for better or for worse. For worse: They've abandoned what used to be a virtually all-burger menu—my favorite involved an entire sleeve of cream cheese basically being smashed between bun and patty—in favor of more alehousey fare. For better: People come in here to cut loose without prejudice; what one wears or drinks to get where she's getting is utterly beside the point.

Upon entry, the Four B's, which advertises itself as "Ballard's Biggest & Best Sports Bar" (they have a thing for alliteration here), looks like a pool hall—and it is, to a degree. But there's plenty of action in back, where an otherwise nondescript interior gives way to a dark, arched-brick area where a typically noisy clientele repairs to drink Jager bombs until their heads spin. Yes, it can get a tad obnoxious, but thankfully the wait staff here, anchored by a 6'6" Andre the Giant type who's been tending bar forever, never let's the bullshit get to a simmer.

The best thing about the Four B's crowd is also the worst. Whereas in certain Ballard bars, you ain't cool unless you've already heard the New Pornographers album that's coming

NORTHWEST · FREMONT

SEATTLE'S BEST DIVE BARS

out three months from now, most of the Four B's patrons are unlikely to know who the New Pornographers even are. Hence, some truly crappy jukebox selections are made—Chili Peppers, Jack Johnson, and Kid Rock crappy. But heck, you don't throw away a Camaro because it's got a dent.

Dive Bar Rating: 🍺🍺🍺🍺

Rickshaw

322 N. 105th St.
Phone: 206-789-0120

The Rickshaw's owner, Ginger Luke, is no ordinary proprietor. She runs a side business called Ginger's Pet Rescue, operating in a bounty hunter-esque industry where private stray gatherers augment and often circumvent a troubled government shelter system. Her restaurant, which usually serves Chinese food, offers American breakfast on weekends and an in-house psychic to read patrons' palms in between turns at the microphone, which is devoted to karaoke seven nights a week.

My buddy Jeff, who lives in Greenwood, is a quintessential Asian-American, which is another way of saying that his idea of seeing live local music is a trip to the nearest karaoke bar. For him, that would mean the Baranof or Yen Wor, which are within walking distance from his home—but he makes an exception for the Rickshaw (which isn't all that far either).

"There are plenty of options in Greenwood if you want to sing a couple songs with friends, but the Rickshaw is the place to go if you want to know where you stand against North Seattle's karaoke elite," says Jeff. "The people there take it seriously and are very good. They offer [karaoke] every night and it's packed with singers until they close—even on Sundays. Patty, the host, has been there for as long as I've been going there, and unlike most of the other k-hosts in the area, she keeps it fun and runs if fairly and efficiently."

"The drinks are stiff and reasonably priced, just like a Greenwood bar needs to be," adds Jeff, who once accompanied me and a national air guitar champion known as Count Rockula (nee Matthew Schwarz) to the Rickshaw to add some unexpected "accompaniment" to the karaoke tracks. When Jeff got up to sing "Jack & Diane"—noting that the single was cut when Mellencamp was "just Cougar"—Rockula was by his side, providing "airaoke" guitar solos in between hand claps.

Like G.E. Smith at a televised tribute concert, Rockula never leaves the stage, providing "airstrumentation" on selections as diverse as "Crazy Train" and "Easy Like Sunday Morning."

"People come up to me and think I'm this professional air guitarist," says Rockula, ordering a vodka drink at last call. "When, in fact, I came up with it in one day."

Dive Bar Rating: 🍺🍺🍺

R. Oscar

Fremont Dock

1102 N. 34th St.
Phone: 206-633-4300

Through its very name, the Fremont Dock provides a visceral reminder of Fremont's—and the entire city's —working waterfront. While civic leaders are quick to tout its bustling port and spectacular ocean views, lost in this hubbub is acknowledgement of the maritime industry that put Seattle on the map in the first place—and remains a vital cog in the city's economy today.

"This is a really industrial city; it just can't see that about itself," says Dave Gering, head of the Manufacturing and Industrial Council of Greater Seattle. "You've got marine infrastructure that cannot be replicated elsewhere."

With marine infrastructure, of course, come marine workers. Gussied up as Ballard has become, this type of professional is still a visible part of the neighborhood fabric. Not so in Fremont, where these folks, while they exist, have been rendered all but invisible, in part because the formerly laid-back Fremont drinking scene has been thoroughly penetrated by yuppies on the make.

The Dubliner used to be a rowdy pub; now it's moved up the hill into modern, sterile digs. The Red Door used to be so narrow you couldn't fit a pregnant woman through it; now it has a warehouse-sized footprint a couple blocks west. The Triangle used to be a pitch-black, beer-only dive with very little breathing room; now it's a sleek ultra-lounge with a really healthy salad menu.

That pretty much leaves the Pacific Inn and Dock (the Buckaroo and 4 B's, too, if they change into tennis shoes after work) to slake the thirst of Fremont's crab trappers and longshoremen. The Dock is about three times the size of the Pac-Inn, with a massive deck that dwarfes its neighbor's by a similar proportion. The woman sitting next to me likes baseball and John McCain, for which she might as well wear a scarlet letter in this, Seattle's most notoriously liberal neighborhood. Near the bar are hung framed photos of burlesque luminaries of yore, and the bartenders wear plenty of perfume. During a shift change, one of them discloses that she spent the day with her kids at the zoo. If there's an upshot to working nights, that'd be it.

Dive Bar Rating:

Jonathan Tuttle

NORTHEAST SEATTLE

LAKE CITY
GREENLAKE
WALLINGFORD
UNIVERSITY DISTRICT

Wedgwood Broiler

In most restaurant-bars, you can actually see the restaurant from the bar, or vice versa. Not at the Wedgwood Broiler, whose restaurant and bar share an address and menu, but breathe very different oxygen. In fact, on any given night, a fair amount of the restaurant patrons actually require mechanical assistance to breathe, period.

The Broiler—the restaurant part—caters mainly to cauliflower heads and the men who love them, if those men are still alive. In a city with a go-go restaurant scene like Seattle's, restaurants that serve liver and onions are in increasingly shorter supply; yet the Broiler has filled that niche for half-a-century.

Wedgwood is a largely white, upper middle class neighborhood in the northeast corner of Seattle. With its tree-lined streets and small-town commercial center, it's more Mayberry than other parts of the city. In Wedgwood, there are three main places to drink—the Broiler, the Wedgwood Alehouse, and the Fiddler's Inn – and only the Broiler serves hard liquor. Hence, by default, the Broiler's dark, cozy lounge is the place to be if hops and barley just won't cut it.

I grew up a block from the Broiler, and when I turned 21, I was anxious to visit the lounge because I wanted to see which of the adults I knew growing up really got after it. A pretty impressive sampling, as it turns out. Although I moved out of the neighborhood after high school, the rest of my family stuck around, so my trips back to my old stomping grounds—and the Broiler—have remained frequent.

Recently, I fulfilled a childhood wish of attempting to eat a 72-ounce steak dinner within an hour. If you fail—and everyone inevitably fails—you owe the restaurant $75. If you succeed, you get...what you just ate, free of charge. Suffice it to say, I came up short, and won't be attempting the feat again, not for awhile anyway. But I will return to the Broiler's bar for free, buttered popcorn and the best Manhattan in town—or at least the best Manhattan in Wedgwood, which, for my first several years on the planet, was the only town I knew.

Dive Bar Rating:

Rose Garden

13717 Lake City Way NE
Phone: 206-365-0465

It should be said here and now that Seattle has no bad neighborhoods, at least not the sort that exist in older cities back east. But it does have bars that would be right at home in bad neighborhoods, and the Rose Garden is one of them.

Bars that don't accept personal checks as a form of payment are common. Bars that have on their menu board the words "no crack pipes or checks" are uncommon. The Rose Garden's menu board boasts such a message, and its customers are a motley crew. There's a guy who looks like Kid from Kid 'n Play seated at one corner of the bar, and another dreadlocked guy who looks like a villain in a Steven Seagal movie at the other. The latter's name is Boogie, and he turns out to be pretty cool, remarking that he's cut down on his drinking lately to "save money on rent"—drunkard's code for what he ends up donating to the Rose Garden in aggregate quaffing fees.

I've been to this place twice, and both times there looked to be at least one exotic dancer enjoying drinks on a regular's dime. Makes sense, considering the Rose Garden is a stone's throw from two strip joints. In Seattle, alcohol is forbidden at flesh palaces, which means the Rose Garden sees more than its fair share of strippers looking to either work up or blow off some steam. It also sees more than its fair share of dudes whose ideal woman is, well, a stripper. In other words, the bar attracts a good amount of aspiring rappers, as evidenced by the freestyle rhyme circles that occasionally form outside the front entrance.

Other than Boogie, the patrons here seem to be in perpetual motion, shuttling between the bathroom and two outdoor areas in between sips of booze (man, they must have small bladders). People here seem, um, agitated—and I have a pretty good idea for why that might be. Hints: It might have something to do with the aforementioned "no checks" sign, as well as another sign near the bathrooms that limits occupancy to one at a time. There's also a woman with a Bluetooth in her ear who's constantly exchanging "low-fives" with certain patrons. You figure it out.

But if exchanging low fives in between frequent forays to the bathroom isn't your bag, there's a lot to like about the Rose Garden. A few of the tables are set up with checker sets, they have Mickey's Hornets (a rarity 'round here) in the cooler, and the cocktails are stiff. Instead of darts in the dart case, there are earrings for sale—and the daytime crowd is older and more into classic soul than the nighttime set, which tends toward raunchy rap. Holla!

Dive Bar Rating: 🍺🍺🍺🍺🍺

Rimrock Steakhouse

With its western mural and thirsty clientele, the Rimrock Steakhouse would feel just as at home in Sheridan, Wyoming as in northeast Seattle, and opens at 6 a.m. every morning, serving 9-to-5 regulars Vegas-priced breakfasts and pre-shift nips. The Rimrock's bar is called the Stirrup room, and it's owned and operated by an erstwhile Wedgwood Broiler waitress named Connie Dunn, who refers to it simply as "a drinking man's bar." The Rimrock's morning bartender is Dunn's longtime boyfriend, Chuck, who told Dunn she was "fucking nuts" when she bought the restaurant 13 years ago.

"This place used to be, if you passed out on the floor with two dollars in your hand, they'd serve you another drink," says Dunn, who was a regular at the Rimrock before she assumed its reins.

While a smattering of younger folks from the neighborhood pop in from time to time, the Rimrock remains one of the last dives to have dodged hipster Seattle's tapeworm-like appetite for authenticity. The bar's strongest weeknight is Wednesday, when a magician named Cliff works the floor for a full hour before a cover band called the Davanos come on. Their repertoire is a mix of country and rock, and they can play virtually everything. But the real draw is their drummer, Fred Holzman.

Holzman has been playing four or five nights per week around town for as long as he can remember. He is a self-taught southpaw who plays on a right-handed kit, and taped to his kick drum is a portrait of the Muppets' drummer, Animal, to whom Holzman is often compared to artistically. Lanky and mustachioed with long, stringy hair and an elastic expressiveness to his face that tends to mesmerize his audience, Holzman looks like the long, lost lovechild of Frank Zappa and Mick Fleetwood, if men could only breed with one another.

Attending a concert with Fred Holzman behind the drums is a forced participatory event. If you're too shy to raise your glass during his "right on" toasts—in which Holzman downs a shot of Rumple Minze, sings the words "right on," and beckons the entire audience to do the same —he will ride your ass from the stage until you cave.

The Rimrock is situated in the heart of Lake City, whose main intersection, NE 125th St. and Lake City Way, boasts a relatively new strip mall that includes a Bartell Drugs, T-Mobile, MoneyTree, a Boeing Employees Credit Union branch, and a Fed-Ex/Kinko's. Whereas on Capitol Hill, a prominent business leader might shit a turkey over such an affront to grassroots retail flavor, the head of Lake City's Chamber of Commerce, Diane Haugen, is ecstatic about these tenants. On Lake City Way, their relative modernity is refreshing to Haugen. Here, what little acreage isn't devoted to car dealerships is occupied by highly specialized, somewhat archaic shops that fix clocks, hawk erotica, and sell model trains or soccer gear (and soccer gear only).

As for the Rimrock, Haugen says simply, "The Rimrock is legendary." And at this legendary haunt, Fred Holzman puts the stir in Stirrup, the rock in Rimrock. Right on, indeed.

Dive Bar Rating: 🍺🍺🍺🍺

Seven Seas

8914 Lake City Way NE
Phone: 206-522-3863

The Seven Seas has long had a gloriously symbiotic relationship with the Shanty, a small, cabin-like tavern located across the parking lot on Lake City Way. Fresh out of college, when I had no money, the metabolism of an Olympic decathlete, and some friends with a large house within walking distance, I used to go to the Shanty frequently, for a few simple reasons: There was rarely any competition for run of the jukebox and pool tables, and beer was cheap (cheap being an especially critical attribute in the life of any 22-year-old). The Shanty experience was, in essence, a virtual carbon copy of what we might have been up to had we chosen to stay in and party, but sometimes you just need a change of scenery. Plus, the Shanty always kept its glassware in the freezer, a masterstroke of customer service that should be emulated by bars worldwide.

Nowadays, the Shanty is for sale, and is only open sporadically, usually on nights when there's live music booked. Next door, the Seven Seas soldiers on. A Chinese restaurant-lounge which provides free delivery to Shanty customers in the mood for something more than pretzels, or liquor to those who need a jolt between pitchers, the Seven Seas' walls are littered with retro-celebrity paraphernalia. (Marilyn Monroe, Elvis Presley, and Ella Fitzgerald are the most popular icons.) Its crowd is a steady stream of lonely old regulars, mostly male and mostly blue collar. One comes up to the square bar, oddly tucked in a nook at the back of the room, orders Rumple Minze with a Bud back, drinks it, and walks out. Apparently he does this every night, says the bartender, Matt.

"You can never have enough good friends," Matt exclaims, and in that spirit, proceeds to pour me a tumbler full of Makers and ice that will "kick [my] ass." It did, and my ass isn't one that's easily kicked.

Dive Bar Rating:

College Inn Pub

4006 University Way NE
Phone: 206-634-2307

Not so much a dive as a dungeon, the College Inn combines the headiness of an English Lit paper with the cheesiness of a medieval restaurant where you drink goat's blood and eat entire cow torsos with your hands. It's also one of the few places that'll drive a man to drink porter.

Porter is the mulatto stepchild of craft beers. It looks as dark as stout, but is nowhere near as thick and creamy. It has the texture of amber ale; but unlike amber ale, it's highly unlikely to quench a workingman's thirst. So where's that leave porter? Collecting dust in the cooler, for the most part.

But porter has its place, and that place would look a lot like the College Inn, whose patrons tend to be either career academics or career drunks (who usually know more than the academics). Porter is a beer for people in the know, who hold this country's ancestral roots across the pond in high esteem. You'd almost never drink porter on a sunny day, just as you'd almost never enter a bar with an underground entrance and no windows, such as the College Inn.

With thick wooden tables randomly stacked atop one another, and random television sets peeking out from random nooks and crannies in random little rooms that might as well be hiding places, the College Inn is a bar best visited after getting a less than flattering mid-term review, when it's 40 degrees and pouring outside and the sun sets at four. It's not a place that will instantly cheer you up, but rather a place for introspection and redoubling. The academic (or drunken) life is a marathon, not a sprint—and porter's the perfect accomplice for such an endeavor.

Dive Bar Rating:

Blue Moon

If blue-collar Seattle is eroding, then the Blue Moon is one of its last vestiges, a tipsy little fly in the world-class ointment. Known coast-to-coast as Seattle's primary bastion of bohemia, the Moon has long served as a magnet to famous literati, including the novelist Tom Robbins, who for years lived in Seattle and still returns frequently from his home an hour-and-a-half north in sleepy LaConner, Wash.

Even before Robbins first set foot in the Moon, he'd become infatuated with the place through word of mouth while living in his native Virginia. "In most cities, there was a bar where beatniks could go and find like-minded people," says Robbins. "In Richmond (Va.), it was the Village; in New Orleans, it was the Seven Seas; in New York, it was the Cedar Tavern; and in Seattle, it was the Moon. So when I moved here in '62, that's the first place I went."

Despite the fact that it's added hard liquor and weathered a pair of potential shut-downs at the hands of encroaching gentrification and overzealous law enforcement types, the Moon's floor is still covered in peanut shells, and its bathrooms still smell like an ocean of fresh piss. Its crowd is a wonderful mélange of artists, writers, gypsies, musicians, transients, trippers, clock-punchers, and brave college students from the nearby University of Washington.

"It's a proletariat and intellectual bar," says Robbins. "You get pipe fitters and carpenters (such as the Moon's current owner, Gus Hellthaler) mingling with grad students and painters. This sort of interchange is healthy. There is a combination of funkiness and earthiness, with a great deal of intellectual and artistic ferment. Seattle has never had a lot of soul, and the Moon is one of the most soulful places in the city."

Robbins was one of a slew of prominent figures—among them *The New Yorker's* Calvin Trillin, Congressman Jim Mc-

Dermott, and Pulitzer Prize-winning poets Carolyn Kizer and Stanley Kunitz—who testified before a Landmarks Board in hopes of saving the Moon from the wrecking ball in 1989. While the pro-Moon contingency's appeal to the Board was unsuccessful, the developers were so moved by the testimony that they extended the bar's lease to 2034, which will mark its centennial celebration.

"The Blue Moon is a cultural treasure," says Robbins. "Every city needs a place like the Blue Moon as an escape valve. In Copenhagen (Germany), there's a part of town where anything goes. When you go into that area, you know you're taking a certain amount of risk. It allows the rest of Copenhagen to be serene and safe."

Concludes Robbins: "Most people are afraid of freedom, and the Blue Moon is a bastion of freedom. When you have a place where people can be themselves to the fullest, it's good for the city, even though they may not realize it."

Dive Bar Rating:

Knarr Shipwreck Lounge

5633 University Way NE
Phone: 206-525-3323

The Knarr is sort of like the Blue Moon's lesser-known, slightly angrier baby brother. You get the same sort of colorful crowd here as you do at the Moon—hippies, bikers, drunks, college kids. But a good portion of floor space is essentially dedicated to billiards, so you also get a healthy sampling of pool sharks here, many of whom carry their own sticks.

The bar takes its name from a type of Viking ship, and sits at the severe north end of University Way, the main commercial strip serving the University of Washington and its surrounding neighborhoods. It's also near Cowan Park and a mile-long wooded trail that leads to Ravenna Park and has long been a homeless hotbed. The Knarr's interior is minimalist, like that of a pool hall, and there are also shuffleboard and darts. The urinals are trough-style, with ice cubes in them to dilute the piss, and the drinks are viciously stiff. And at the Knarr, tension between long-hairs and college boys is s a good deal thicker than at the Moon, where everybody just seems to get along, man.

There used to be bars along "the Ave" (this being the commonly-used nickname for University Way) students could get into with fake ID—then there was the Knarr. At the Knarr, you didn't need any ID. And yet the place never seemed to get busted.

I couldn't tell you if they have food at the Knarr. That's not what the Knarr's for. While turnover on the Ave. has traditionally been far higher than in other parts of the city, the Knarr has been that rare constant, an anomaly drenched in anarchy. Perhaps there are some people who aren't so afraid of freedom after all.

Dive Bar Rating: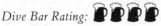

Dante's

5300 Roosevelt Way NE
Phone: 206-525-1300

When one of America's best-looking serial killers is said to have seduced his first victim at your bar many years ago, you can either embrace the notoriety or close your doors for good. Dante's has shrewdly chosen the former approach, devoting a healthy amount of wall space to news clippings about Ted Bundy's 1974 abduction of Lynda Ann Healy. Bundy was a frequenter of Dante's back in the '70s, and it should come as no surprise: The place is essentially a playful ode to devilishness, with its front room set aside as a de facto shrine to Dante's Inferno.

The rest of the cavernous bar is rather disjointed and medieval. There's an upper level where engineering students compete in boat races after finishing mid-terms, and a lower "dungeon" with darts and such. Bar games are everywhere, and there's a giant oak table near the Inferno room where hungry patrons can complement their chosen hooch with any number of deep-fried snacks on Dante's menu (if fried food isn't your thing, you're shit out of luck).

There are people who claim that the University of Washington lacks a consistently good bar within walking distance of campus, and not without reason. But these people have apparently never been to Dante's, which, back when I attended UW, was known as the place to hold someone's 21 run, because the bartenders wouldn't cut the primary celebrant off—even after she hurled. Someone would just clean up the puke, the celebrant would "rally," and things would carry on as though the vomit were a mere speed bump on the road to debauched adulthood.

Customers don't really come here to hang out and have a beer; they come here to get hammered. It's hard to imagine a worse bar for a first date, unless your intentions are sleazier than most first dates—like Ted Bundy's obviously were.

Dive Bar Rating: 🍺🍺🍺

Back Door Pub

12330 Lake City Wy.
Phone: 206-364-2642

Heading southbound on Bothell Way the day after Thanksgiving, a peculiar amount of patrol cars could be spotted pulling over drivers they presumed to be intoxicated on one of the most notorious drunken driving nights of the year. This could help explain why Lake City's Back Door Pub is unusually quiet, more reminiscent of a Monday than a Friday, says a burly, bald bartender named Chad, who usually works Mondays.

Chad has been guzzling coffee and cranberry juice intermittently, beads of sweat noticeable on his forehead. He proclaims that he's sufficiently hopped up for a weekend night's work. "All I need is for 40 people to walk in the door," he adds.

Thanksgiving night, that precise thing happened, with a post-midnight rush that had Chad "making Washington Apples faster than people could order them." As an older fellow with a Texas drawl sips Budweiser and reads a paperback at the bar, Chad predicts that once people awaken from their triptophan comas brought on by the ingestion of leftover turkey, a similar plot might soon unfold.

About all there is to eat are $1.50 hot dogs, and the jukebox is dominated by the likes of the Marshall Tucker Band, George Thorogood, and AC/DC. Other than more signs referencing pirates than your average neighborhood dive, the Backdoor is just that: your average neighborhood dive, the ideal complement to the showier Rimrock a couple doors down.

Dive Bar Rating: 🍺🍺🍺

Cabin Tavern

19322 Richmond Beach Drive
Phone:206-542-1177

The Cabin is in Richmond Beach, which in the early 20th Century used to be a community of summer homes owned by Seattleites seeking tranquil shoreline respite from life in the big city. Funny thing is, Seattle wasn't such a big city back then, and Richmond Beach is only about 10 minutes north of the current city limit. Today, Richmond Beach is a suburb that's considered to be very conveniently located in proximity to Seattle's metro core. Funny how times change; funnier still how the Cabin hasn't really changed, which is why we're going to use our Get Out of Seattle Free card to annex this wonderful little bar into this book.

I dream often of the perfect tavern. It is unpretentious. It's at least half-full on a lazy Sunday afternoon, with sports on TV. It's in the middle of nowhere—preferably near a body of water—yet not too far from anywhere. It has cheap food, regionally-produced beer, a secluded patio, and a low ceiling.

The Cabin has all of these things. It is as close to a dream tavern as I can imagine—only this tavern has hard booze, and for some reason, the tartar sauce here tastes better than just about anywhere else.

Two things are especially unusual about the Cabin. For one, the floor is sloped, which can lead to a face plant for the well-lubed. Furthermore, the Cabin is smack in the middle of a residential block, a peculiarity that stands in defiance of modern-day zoning regulations that dates back to the community's original incarnation as a laid-back beach getaway.

If you don't know where the Cabin is, you're not going to find it, as it sits at the bottom of a steep, serpentine path that feels more like a Puget Sound boat launch than a road. Most of the time, it functions as an affable neighborhood watering hole. But during breaks from school, the Cabin becomes a temporary hotspot for tipplers looking to reacquaint themselves with the glories of their relative youth in a place that feels like home.

Dive Bar Rating:

Sylvia's Little Red Hen

7115 Woodlawn Ave. NE
Phone: 206-522-1168

The Little Red Hen is antithetical to smug, urbane, indie rock-in' Seattle—times three. First of all, people partner-dance here, which rarely happens anywhere else in a city known for its arms-folded, head–bobbing manner of observing live music. Secondly, the Hen is Seattle's lone purebred country music bar—not alt-country like the Tractor Tavern, but Alan Jackson-LeeAnn Womack-George Strait, middle-of-the-country country. Thirdly, it's a whiskey-soaked, deep-fried, dust-covered, shit-kickin', steel-toed liver pulverizer in Seattle's healthiest neighborhood, Greenlake.

After 9, the Hen plays host to a generationally-diverse group of Caucasians, coupled up and two-stepping to the sounds of the Rainieros, Shadrack, or the Joe Slick Band. The lights are lit low, and a meticulous western mural covers the bar's southernmost wall. But in the hours leading up to and through happy hour, the Hen is largely populated by blue-collar regulars and neighborhood denizens who are drawn by the bar's reliably stiff pours and the culinary stylings of Irwin, the Filipino chef.

The Hen's bar is called the Mirror Room, so named because it's ringed by an overhead mirror. While the bar's long-time manager, Connie Robertson, is the stone-faced portrait of efficiency, a recent Wednesday evening saw a shift hand-off between a tramp-stamped vixen in black western leathers and an earth-mother type in a frilly dress and Schmidt t-shirt. (The Hen doesn't serve Schmidt, but it should.)

Irwin's menu tends not toward the cuisine of his native country, but rather toward $9.50 steak and onion entrees and stuffed green peppers, his signature dish. As for the crowd, there are two middle-aged guys, one of whom works for a railroad company, trying to convince a younger guy to work for City Light once he gains journeyman status. Seated at a table near the bar is a skinny, fifty-something man named Bob, who remarks to his companion that he sure could use a woman in his life right about now, a line fit for a country song. While he's far from rude, Bob is a skittish chap, constantly hopping out of his seat to order a beer, darting to the bathroom, or playfully badger the bartenders, who seem a trifle annoyed by his antics. Bob introduces himself to one of the blue-collar gabbers, leaves, comes back five minutes later, and introduces himself again. In a patronizing tone, Bob's counterpart wishes him a happy New Year and slowly walks away.

Dive Bar Rating:

Changes

2103 N. 45th St.
Phone: 206-545-8363

Long known simply as the only gay bar north of the Lake Washington Ship Canal, Changes made national news a couple years ago when, during one of its karaoke nights, a young woman violently attacked a male patron. His crime? Singing "Yellow" by Colplay, a song so loathed by the female patron that mere cat-calls just wouldn't do.

A *Seattle P-I* clip recounting the incident is framed and hung near the entryway in this tiny, narrow bar, which is aesthetically evocative of the Green Lantern, a late, great Wallingford dive that did brisk business selling kegs to anyone who could present picture ID, irrespective of whether it said they were 21. What differentiates Changes from the Lantern has little to do with looks, and everything to do with predominantly male clientele's preference for whispering sweet nothings into the ears of other men. But aside from that precondition and the rainbow color scheme of Changes' logo, the only thing that will tip you off to the fact that it's a gay bar is the music, which tilts stereotypically toward Rihanna and Beyonce remixes. Other than that, there are pull tabs, softball trophies, a pool table, and plasma screens tuned to sports.

According to Herb Hudson, a longtime fixture of the Wallingford drinking scene, Changes was once a more heterosexual bar known as the Rathole. Ironically, this is actually a far better name for a gay bar than Changes, which might give passersby the mistaken impression that people magically "change" into homosexuals. But figuratively, the name harkens back to a bygone era when gay men were terrified to come out; hence, when they did, it represented a major transitional period in terms of how they presented themselves to the world and how the world responded to their newfound public identity. The gay rights movement still has a long way to go, but boy has it come a long way since then. Amen to that—and to Changes' all-day Sunday happy hour, which runs from 11 a.m. 'til close.

Dive Bar Rating: 🍺🍺

Duchess Tavern

2827 NE 55th St.
Phone: 206-527-8606

A Northeast Seattle and University of Washington institution, the Duchess is the rarest of creatures: the white-collar dive (in fairness, dive is more a state of mind than anything else here, as the Dutch's upkeep is pretty pristine). Here, doctors, lawyers, brokers, writers, professors, and students commiserate before Husky home games or during class reunions, eschewing swankier establishments in favor of the Duchess' congenial feel, no-bullshit pub grub, and spacious gaming parlor.

Situated across the street from a cemetery and just north of University Village, the Duchess is also known for its "Beer Hunter's Club," into which no one can be inducted until he or she has consumed every beer on the Duchess' vast brew menu, which runs some 40 brands strong. Staffed primarily by guys you want to call "dad," it's one of the few bars in town where it feels normal to ingest a pitcher of domestic lager and a burger before 10 a.m. on a Saturday ("UW Beer," a mystery tap that's usually Hamm's or the like, goes for around $3 a pitcher). Another nice touch: television sets in the bathrooms, with that day's sports page tacked to bulletin boards above the urinals.

The Duchess has its detractors, namely hipster transplants who are thrown by the Dutch's chummy, classic rock vibe. The bar can also get a tad obnoxious on nights when undergrads take over en masse. To the former quibble: Sorry the Dutch reminds you of everybody's favorite Thursday night bar (except yours) in the small Midwestern town you went to college in, and sorry you weren't born here. To the latter: The Dutch is walking distance from campus; deal with it. For those who have no beef with the Dutch: Good for you, and yes, you should order a twelfth pitcher.

Dive Bar Rating:

SEATTLE'S BEST DIVE BARS

Leny's Place

2219 N. 56th St.
Phone: 206-632-9175

Yep, there's really only one "n" in this Leny's name. Yet while the name's remained the same, the bar has not. What used to be a tobacco-stained flytrap with crusty regulars, pool hustlers, and budget beer is now a full-service dive bar, with multiple TVs tuned to sports and, hard booze, and a scrumptious dinner menu imported from Bad Albert's, a Ballard bar whose Dock Street Burger ranks among the area's finest.

The miracle of Leny's makeover is the subtlety with which it's been undertaken. Those crusty regulars and pool hustlers still flock to the bar for cheap ($4) 32-ounce tankards of Rainier, and the infusion of sporty, clean-cut youngsters hasn't created much friction with the old guard. Leny's crowd is basically a Greek Row version of nearby Al's, mindful of the fact that they're basically entering the living room of a bunch of people who've been living there a lot longer than they have.

The trick to Leny's is that while it's added certain amenities, it hasn't gone overboard to the point where it's shed its well-worn skin. Witness the men's bathroom, which still ranks upon the foulest in town. Hence, Leny's lesson is that you don't need to trick out a place in order to bolster its bottom line. Rather, you're better off accentuating its hard-earned charms, craggy as they may be.

Dive Bar Rating: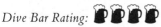

Al's Tavern

Herb Hudson is the consummate veteran of the Wallingford tavern scene. He tended bar at Andy's before it became Murphy's, the Rathole before it became Changes, and Al's before it became…Al's, that rare bar that's remained more or less intact despite passing through the hands of several owners, including Hudson himself.

Sharing a city block with an Indian restaurant and the Erotic Bakery (for those unaware of this Seattle landmark, frosted nipples and cocks are commonplace atop a cake made here), Al's has operated contiguously since the '40s, and doesn't promote its presence beyond a tiny sandwich board parked on the sidewalk out front and a couple generic neon signs—"cold beer," "cocktails"—in the window. As for the interior, Hudson, who owned Al's for 12 years while simultaneously serving as its nighttime bartender, reports that about the only change he's seen is the shortening of the bar so as to usher in a pair of pool tables (unfortunately, a shuffleboard table was also jettisoned to make way for the felt). And on the wall is a mural, painted in 1972 by local artist Phil Hendrickson, which traces the evolution of nearby Shilshole Bay from prehistoric to modern times.

About 10 years ago, Hudson sold Al's to a group that included current co-owner Max Genereaux, who also runs the Sunset Tavern, a popular rock club on Ballard Avenue. Genereaux's business partner is Marie Fultz, a contemporary of Hudson's, who once worked under him at Al's and bartended at various locations on the street for some 30 years (having hung up her apron, she now handles Genereaux's books). There are corn dogs and "salty nut sacks" on Al's menu, Cazadores shots are a mere $5, and the soundtrack is a tasteful mix of indie rock (Built to Spill), classic rock (the Stones), and country (Will Oldham). There are playing cards stuck to the ceiling – the aftermath of multiple appearances by a magician by the name of Cliff Gustafson—and when the Seahawks or Huskies score a touchdown, the price of Rainier drops to 25 cents a schooner.

There are people like Hudson, a goateed old tough who wears a thick flannel and his hair slicked back, who've been frequenting Al's for the better part of half-a-century. Genereaux is extremely respectful of these folks, and the hipsters who inevitably meander in after 10 clearly adhere to the owner's set of values, treating the regulars not as ironic curiosities, but instead as barstool deities, from whom much wisdom can be patiently gleaned.

Dive Bar Rating:

Moon Temple

Long Island Iced Teas are never good idea. They're not a good idea to kickstart a night, because after two or three of them, the average drinker's night will either be over or on a one-way train to Blackoutsville. They're not a good idea in the middle of the night—the alcoholic's equivalent to dripping liquid acid onto a bowl of pot. And they're definitely not a good idea toward the end of the night, unless you want to go out like John Bonham.

The Moon Temple's do-it-all (I can't recall ever seeing another employee) proprietor/bartender, John, doesn't make Long Island Iced Teas. Instead, he's the master of what we'll call John Island Iced Teas, various secret potions containing any number of different liquors that sound like they should taste horrible but instead taste like tropical punch.

The best drink order one can make at the Moon Temple is to ask John to fix whatever he wants, and ask him not to tell you what you're about to drink until after you've drank it. He views this as a challenge, and is bound to bring his A-game to the drink, both in terms of mixology and potency. The drink inevitably tastes as though it contains no liquor. Posthumous-ly, you find out that it contained nothing but liquor. Simply put, the Moon Temple serves the stiffest mixed drinks in all of Seattle, provided you're willing to let John do his thing instead of ordering your trusty Cape Cod.

In terms of ambiance, the Moon Temple is one of those Chinese restaurant-lounges that would be better off ceasing the charade that is their restaurant and focusing exclusively on sating its juicier clientele. The food is respectable; it's a tossup as to whether you're better off coating your drunken stomach with General Tso's Chicken here or a Dick's Deluxe down the road. The bar is dark and simple, with a pair of TVs typically tuned to the game of the night and a Buddha statue in one corner. There are random depictions of karate warriors and dragons on the walls that look more like rubber stamps than paintings, and there's a weird back room between the bar and the bathrooms that's almost always empty and looks as though it could be put to better use as an after-hours gambling parlor. Consider that a suggestion, John, if you aren't already there yet.

Dive Bar Rating: 🍺🍺🍺🍺

Goldie's on 45th

2121 N. 45th St.
Phone: 206-632-3453

For such a white, yuppified, family neighborhood, Wallingford's main drag, N. 45th Street, features a ton of dives, including Goldie's, a bar that I last walked into during Boston's miraculous comeback from a 7-0 deficit in the 2008 American League Championship Series. I swear the previous time I was there, they'd installed a fireplace near the entrance in an effort to draw in a more moneyed clientele. If that gambit ever existed, it's since ceased, as the vibe has been dialed back to that of classic dark, divey sports bar with lots of dartboards and pool tables. To this end, there's a generous amount of room to move in Goldie's, but the ceiling is quite low and there are wooden beams aplenty, giving it the feeling of drinking in a roadside lodge with nothing but forest out back.

On this particular Thursday night, Goldie's happy hour patrons are an odd collection. There's a lonely old guy mumbling to himself and consuming a pitcher without any assistance. There's a black guy with a Tom Brady jersey on, and a white guy with a shirt which reads, "I'm Rick James, bitch!" (Shouldn't they switch?) As the game wears on, a group of hippie gals rolls in to play darts. It's ladies night, after all.

Thankfully, the Red Sox comeback in that game would not lead to yet another 21st Century trip to the World Series, as the Devil Rays took care of business in the decisive Game 7. It seems hard to fathom now, given Boston's recent success, but there was a time not too long ago when the team was mired in a hundred-year drought, and its fans were considered among the most sympathetic figures in sports. Just look at those fuckers now: Cocky and mouthy as Yankee fans, with an ever-increasing fair weather bandwagon that gobbles up precious real estate during the team's every road game. It's really amazing how short certain people's memories are—here's hoping that the next hundred-year drought starts sooner rather than later.

Dive Bar Rating: 🍺🍺🍺🍺

North City Tavern

17554 15th Ave. NE
Phone: 206-362-1443

Forgive me for extending the Seattle city limit by a mile or two, but to give the North City Tavern anything less than a full-throated treatment here would be a far greater sin. Its name sounds like the sort of place where Starsky and Hutch would meet Huggy Bear, and its décor hasn't been updated much beyond the year that show went off the air.

Walking into the North City is like crashing a party in the basement of an unfamiliar neighbor who perpetually has three broken down Buicks parked on his front lawn. On the karaoke mike is a small black woman in a raincoat, butchering "Hotel California." The furniture is a collection of office chairs, mismatched tables, and shabby couches. While there aren't more than a couple pool tables here, the folks who play on them are serious enough to bring their own sticks. The wallpaper is maritime-themed, and the bathrooms are down a couple steps from the rest of the bar, the sort of quirk that goes unnoticed until after six or seven beers, at which point those stairs might as well be road spikes.

But back to *Starsky & Hutch*: this appears to actually be a bar where cops hang out. To wit, a wiseacre regular signs a couple lawmen up to karaoke "I Got You Babe." (The karaoke here is called "Larryoke", a peculiar moniker given that the KJ is female.) The cops are good sports about their homoerotic pairing, and give way to an old boozer who can't be bothered to get up from his stool. No matter: The KJ hands him the mike at the bar, which isn't all that far from the staging area. He proceeds to belt out a respectable version of Otis Redding's "Dock of the Bay," a fitting anthem for a bar where nobody's in a hurry to do much of anything, except maybe tie one on.

Dive Bar Rating: 🍺🍺🍺🍺🍺

Old 5th Avenue Tavern

8507 5th Ave. NE
Phone: 206-522-1515

When Tara Burkett bought the Old 5th Ave. Tavern in 1995, she says it catered to "more of an older crowd, with pull tabs." Like the Reservoir up the road, it served only beer (wine was available, albeit as an afterthought) and didn't concern itself much with décor.

Burkett, who'd spent the five years prior to her purchase working for a fish processor in Alaska, set about making subtle changes. She kept the pull tabs and free pool intact, but dimmed the lights and added liquor (the Rez has liquor too now). She also updated the jukebox to reflect her hard-rock tastes. Still, Burkett says, "It took quite a few years to pull in a younger crowd." But she's finally achieved that (granted, it can tend toward a full-scale sausage fest) without scaring off the regulars, a tricky endeavor if there ever was one. And to reward her hungry clientele, she serves 50-cent tacos on Tuesday.

Taco Tuesday is hardly a novel concept. In fact, for most people, it will conjure up memories of grammar school cafeterias, and bars like West Seattle's Rocksport offer similar specials. But two things are exceptional about the 5th Ave's Taco Tuesday: (1) The Jimmy Carter-era pricing (the Rocksport's tacos cost a buck apiece—still a great deal but still twice the price of the Fifth Ave's), and (2) the speed with which Burkett serves her shells. The explanation for the latter is easy: Burkett assembles the tacos behind the bar herself. She scoops the meat out of a crock pot, and keeps the (hard) casing warm in a toaster oven. You'll have the essentials of your meal delivered within a minute, and then you'll have a very short walk to the condiment bar. So tiny is the 5th Ave that you're liable to be dodging pool cues as you shovel tomatoes and cheese atop your ground beef.

My brother Joe no longer drinks. When he did drink, the

5th Ave. was his favorite bar. When I ask him what he misses most about drinking, it's not the drinking he misses; it's the 5th Ave., which he succinctly describes as "bromantic."

"Where else in the neighborhood could you go to drink $3 shots washed down with $3 pitchers, watch the Mariners back when they mattered, and listen to Radiohead's Amnesiac at the same time?" he adds. "La dolce vita!"

Dive Bar Rating:

Reservoir Bar

8509 Roosevelt Way NE
Phone: 206-526-9737

There are certain bars you walk into that are openly hostile to people who shave more than once a week. The Reservoir, so named because it's located across the street from a reservoir, used to be one of those bars. It had a pop-a-shot game, domestic beer and….that was it. Bars like this are like private clubs for folks whose wages come by the hour. The reverse snobbery that exists in places like this will probably cease around the time that snobbery itself exists—which will probably be never.

Except the Reservoir isn't really one of these places anymore. A few years ago, the Reservoir began serving hard booze. With hard booze came an influx of younger drinkers—some female, even—and with that, a sundeck, spruced-up interior, and better food. Today, the Maple Leaf watering hole hangs on to its dive bar status by the slightest of threads, and mostly because what it once was (and because of its green-and-white retro exterior, which has remained intact).

The Reservoir's good fortune mirrors that of northeast Seattle, save for Lake City. In Wedgwood, for instance, what once was a medieval-looking dump called the Wedgwood Inn is now the Wedgwood Alehouse, which features artisan food, rotating microbrew tap handles, trivia nights, and insufferable service. Further down 35th Ave. NE, the Fiddler's Inn has remained the same in name and marquee only (its presence is signaled by a rusty fiddle, high in the sky). But what once was a dank, smoke-filled beer hall with floor-to-ceiling carpet is now a mellow, rustic-chic fleece and flannel hangout with open mike night, a patio garden, and pesto pizza.

Like a lot of these places, the Reservoir is still a fun place to kick back with friends and neighbors. But it's neither unique nor intimidating, not anymore.

Dive Bar Rating:

Teddy's Tavern

1012 NE 65th St.
Phone:206-526-9174

A scruffy Sam Elliott to the Duchess' Patrick Swayze, Teddy's is just as likely to play host to a Sunday afternoon convoy of Harley enthusiasts as it is a post-rugby lager scrum. With the vintage visage of Teddy Roosevelt, monocle and all, hanging above its entrance, Teddy's is a bar named for a neighborhood named for a street named for a President—but I've always liked to imagine it was named for the nearby high school that shares Ted's surname as well.

Like any public school, Roosevelt High has its fair share of students with modest means. But more than any other tax-payer-funded school in Seattle, it boasts a plethora of students with immodest means, kids from Laurelhurst or View Ridge who could throw parties fit for the Rockefellers and Astors of the world. I played Little League with these kids, and while none of us have succeeded at becoming professional athletes, most of us have succeeded at becoming professional drinkers.

Hence, in my imagination, I like to picture these Roughrider comrades visiting Teddy's in between homeroom and Home Ec, a flannel-and-jeans version of *Gossip Girl*. Instead of attending fashion shows or sitting courtside at Knicks games, my co-stars would play beer pong on Teddy's back patio, standing tableside for their own games. Instead of Dom, my crew's drinking Full Sail. Instead of John Legend, they're listening to John Prine. And instead of being driven from club to club in black sedans, they bribe freshmen into ferrying them from house party to house party in used Suburbans. Hey Hollywood, any takers?

Dive Bar Rating: 🍺🍺

SEATTLE'S BEST DIVE BARS

Caroline Tavern

13702 15th Ave. NE
Phone: 206-363-3300

If you blink as you pass by it, you might miss the fact that the Caroline Tavern is a tavern and not simply a house. It looks exactly like a house, and is located in a neighborhood where there is nothing but houses. It actually is a residence: A maintenance man lives upstairs. But downstairs is a small, durable drinking establishment, which can best be described aesthetically as a ski resort watering hole for people who can't afford lift tickets.

It could also be described as a country club bar for people who can't afford a country club membership, as Jackson Park Golf Course, one of the city's three public golf courses, is located directly across the street, making Caroline's the perfect place for workaday duffers to quaff cheap cans of Hamm's. The men's room is clean, but the stall has no door and the crapper is maybe two feet from the sink, making mid-dump how-do-you-dos a very real threat. It's the sort of bar where regulars commiserate at all hours; one afternoon, a woman burst in and shouted at her husband: "You sold the cabinet, didn't you, you dirty fuck? You sold the cabinet so you could get drunk again, you motherfucker!" She then left and slammed the door.

Long after the links close, it serves as a neighborhood meeting place for blue-collar workers of all stripes. The night we were there, a group of Middle Eastern cab drivers shot pool and drank Rainier, and the bartender's sister brought in a tray of homemade chocolate brownies for customers to enjoy. A power outage afflicted the rest of the neighborhood, but somehow the lights kept flickering at Caroline's.

The Caroline Tavern has been around since 1933, and bears the distinction of being the site of one of Will Rogers' last meals. In 1935, Rogers was in town with his buddy Wiley Post, and before a scheduled engagement at the posh Washington Athletic Club downtown, Rogers is said to have enjoyed a meal at Caroline's. That summer, he decided to take a ride in an experimental aircraft owned by Post, a respected aviator. The engine failed and the plane crashed in Alaska, killing both men.

Dive Bar Rating:

DOWNTOWN SEATTLE

DOWNTOWN
BELLTOWN
QUEEN ANNE
CHINATOWN
SODO

Joe's

5th Ave. & S. King St.
Phone # not listed

Upon entering Joe's, a shabby oasis of downtrodden Americana in Seattle's bustling Chinatown, I'm greeted by two drunkards—one white, one Mexican—about to duke it out over the color of one another's skin. With the Marshall Tucker Band providing the only semblance of noise in an otherwise silent bar, the two would-be combatants end up hugging instead.

"I was cool before cool was cool," says the white guy, exiting the bar with one of the most incomprehensibly awesome one-liners I've ever heard.

In the annals of bar snobbery, there are two common types: One is when you've got a really swank bar where people look askance at those whose grooming habits don't mesh with the pages of *GQ* or *Elle*, the other is when you've got a down-home watering hole where those who walk in with ironed pants and a fresh shave are greeted with "what the fuck are you doing here" looks from the regulars. A lot of the bars in this book fit into the latter category, but very few of them fit into a third category, where if you aren't homeless, you aren't cool. Joe's is of this final realm.

During lunch hour in the middle of the week, the bar is populated by maybe a dozen patrons. The smell of unwashed ass and armpit sweat in the air is so thick I could cut it, but that's par for the course at Joe's. I take a seat and order a beer. Next to me is an old, two-bit drunk named Tom, who immediately launches into a profane tirade about how neither Obama nor McCain will be good for the country, because neither of them are from the great State of Washington.

Once he settles down and stops inadvertently spitting in my beer, I learn that Tom grew up a few blocks from my boyhood home in Wedgwood and attended the same Catholic grade and high schools as I. Usually, when you find such commonality with a stranger, it's a wonderful thing. But looking at Tom, I couldn't help but think that if things were to break a certain way for me—given my taste for hooch and lack of technical acumen outside my flagging profession—I could end up just like him. And that wasn't a pretty thought.

Dive Bar Rating:

Turf Restaurant & Lounge

200 Pike St.
Phone: 206-682-2324

Located underneath a large cement parking garage a city block from Pike Place Market, the Turf—easily identified by a vertical sign that has "TURF" spelled out in bold green lettering—has long served as a safe haven for freelance street salesman who, were they to go about their day's business al fresco, would be stationery targets for police officers, warranted or otherwise. It *Do the Right Thing* were filmed in Seattle, the Turf would have been a primary location. Wary be the tourist who accidentally stumbles into this place, which used to be located even closer to the Market before a now-closed Johnny Rockets franchise forced it on down the road.

During lunch, there are as many construction workers wolfing down hot beef sandwiches and teriyaki as there are flashier types. (The also have oxtail and a host of highly unusual, ridiculously cheap items on the menu). At the dusty, institutional back bar, an elderly female bartender whom everyone refers to reverently takes care of business. But once work lets out, an Asian bartender with a stud earring who doesn't take shit off of anybody assumes the reins; he's not amused when a cat with a velour tracksuit on tries to pay for his tallboy with a $1.75 bus voucher.

At happy hour, R&B permeates the jukebox, and the crowd is mostly middle-aged black folk. Most of them double-fist: a liquor drink and beer for backup. As an Isley Brothers ditty comes on, two nattily-dressed gentlemen begin arguing about women. Things escalate to where they have to be physically restrained—even the bartender's death stare won't stop them from getting at one another's throats. But eventually, they do the right thing: They chill.

Dive Bar Rating:

Double Header

Up until about the turn of the 21st Century, Pioneer Square's Double Header was believed to be the nation's longest continuously-operating gay bar. Today, gay patrons are hard to come by at the Double Header, to the point where it's not really considered a gay bar anymore (still, the occasional local gay politician will hold an election night party here, for symbolism's sake). In fact, patrons in general are pretty hard to come by at the Double Header, a spacious dive near one of Seattle's most notorious open-air drug markets that appears to be a shell of its raucous, trailblazing self.

Occasionally, however, the Double Header reveals its roots. For one, there's a wall display devoted to the '70s-era exploits of Ze Whiz Kidz, a seminal drag queen cabaret act that influenced punk rock and performance art as much as it did local gay culture. And the crowd appears to be mostly dudes—homeless dudes, who presumably waltz in from any number of nearby shelters. On one visit, I witnessed a downtrodden guy work himself into such a tizzy over his lost wallet that the cops had to be summoned. They're never far away in this neck of the woods, which sits on the rough easterly edge of Pioneer Square's bridge and tunnel district.

Then there was the time a patron offered a friend of mine "dinner and a movie." While neither of us took this literally to mean he wanted James to join him at his abode for beef stroganoff and a screening of *Annie Hall*, we had no idea what the slang meaning of the phrase was. The next day, an area homosexual informed me that the guy wanted to exchange drugs (dinner) for a movie (blow job). It seems as though the Double Header hasn't completely lost sight of its cock-tastic youth after all.

Dive Bar Rating:

Kelly's

It's an ominous sign when you approach a bar and there's a paddy wagon parked across the street. It's even more ominous sign when such an occurrence isn't all that rare at said bar. Welcome to Kelly's, the most frightening drinking establishment in Seattle.

On the surface, what separates Kelly's from its main rivals (Dome Stadium Tavern, Joe's, Turf, Rose Garden, Fortune Sports Bar) for this dubious honor is its friendly, Irish name and shamrock façade. Upon approach, this doesn't look to be the sort of bar that attracts mercurial street urchins, but that's exactly what it is. If you walk through Kelly's doors looking half-presentable, conversations are liable to come to an immediate halt, with the shocked looks on people's eyes asking a very blunt question: "What the fuck are you doing in here?"

This isn't so much reverse snobbery as it is suspicion that you might be an undercover cop, as the Belltown of today is filled with trendy restaurants, high-rise condo towers, and the people who can afford them. But the Belltown of yesterday—not World War II yesterday, but through the first Bush Presidency yesterday—was Seattle's skid row, an area rife with junkies, dealers, pimps, hookers, crooks, and various other ne'er-do-wells. The park across the street from Kelly's used to be the city's most notorious open-air drug market; now it's an off-leash dog park for well-heeled urban dwellers. Or at least it's supposed to be, as most of the folks who should be giving Scruffy a few hot laps are still scared shitless of the corner.

If Kelly's sticks out like a sort thumb in today's Belltown, it's only because it's outlasted its contemporaries. Hence, the tendency for neighborhood riffraff to congregate at the last relic standing can hardly be unexpected. Taken in this context, is Kelly's a victim of its own survival, a gnarly needle in a haughty haystack? That's for you to decide, if you dare.

Dive Bar Rating: 🍺🍺🍺🍺🍺

5-Point Cafe

415 Cedar St.
Phone: 206-448-9993

Within five minutes of walking into the 5-Point, Alice in Chains or Soundgarden will play loudly on the jukebox. The female cocktail waitress will be angsty, pale, and pierced, and the male bartender burly, stoic, and tattooed. Whiskey and sodas will be mixed as though whoever took your order developed temporary hearing loss when you uttered the words "and soda," and the customer-to-black-leather-jacket ratio will be roughly 2-to-1.

It will be gray, cold, and rainy outside (even if it isn't, you'll feel a though it is), and there will be a corner booth occupied by a pair of transient drunks, who will be permitted to drink until they pass out or break something. In the men's room, the toilet seat will be rimmed with dried-up piss, puke, or granola (hard to tell which is which sometimes), there may or may not be tissue or soap, and ballpoint vandalism is not only tolerated—it's encouraged.

If you'd like to stay past last call, that's fine, because the 5-Point doubles as a 24-hour diner (there's also a Laundromat that shares its name next door). And if you like hashbrowns, you need only order them once, as your server will keep them coming as long as you keep eating.

In short, the 5-Point is a grunge time machine; the only difference between the 5-Point circa 1989 and the 5-Point now is that you can't smoke indoors anymore—which is a shame, because time machines really should be exempted from laws that don't suit their era.

Dive Bar Rating: 🍺🍺🍺🍺🍺

Ozzie's

105 W. Mercer St.
Phone: 206- 284-4618

The transformation of Ozzie's from a cavernous dive bar to a hotspot for Greek system hookups is one of the more phenomenal in Seattle nightlife history. What makes it so amazing is Ozzie's has done very little to invite such a changing of the guard. Sure, it's added an auxiliary bar and a small rooftop deck, but the interior still looks as though it's been decorated by an alcoholic clown, karaoke still rules the stereo, and there's a fully operational shower in the upstairs bathroom. One of these days, I'm going to show up with a towel and a change of underwear, order two bottles of beer, and then take a 15-minute shower, just to see how (if?) people react. Who knows: If you did it at 1 a.m. on a Friday, you might get a hot, wet blow-j, just for being in the right place at the right time.

But I prefer the Ozzie's of my youth, where more than a few patrons showed up with all their belongings in a couple plastic grocery bags, and the hottest slice of ass in the joint resembled Phyllis Diller. At Ozzie's B.A.B.S. (Before Axe Body Spray), the crowd was sufficiently small to stage karaoke in the bar instead of the dining room, and pizza that tasted awful while sober tasted positively phenomenal after a dozen salty dogs.

My favorite Ozzie's story actually stems from a night in my twenties when I was imbibing elsewhere. Half a dozen of my closest friends were tearing shit up like usual on a Saturday when a rough-looking guy near the pool tables started talking shit to the burliest of the bunch. They almost came to blows a couple times through the course of the evening, but ultimately resisted. Eventually, the shit-talker stumbled to his truck, which was parked next to a dumpster in a nearby parking lot.

My pals poured out shortly after last call, and happened across the lippy patron, passed out cold in his truck. Ah, sweet revenge: they managed to lift the dumpster up off the ground and drop it into the back of the guy's pickup. At that point, he woke up and hollered; but by then, the damage was done.

Ozzie's B.A.B.S. also served as a great place to lube up before Sonic games, simply because most fans would flock to hotter spots like Peso's, Jalisco, T.S. McHugh's, or Floyd's, leaving Ozzie's wide open. Now the Sonics are gone, and so too is the Ozzie's of my youth.

Dive Bar Rating: 🍺🍺🍺

R. Oscar

The Funhouse

206 5th Ave. N.
Phone: 206- 374-8400

If the 5-Point ditched its diner side and decided to accommodate live music, odds are it would end up looking a lot like the Funhouse, which sits a couple blocks away from its grungy forerunner and boasts the same black and white checkered floor.

Boasting a gigantic, scary clown face above its front door, the Funhouse serves as a welcome antidote to the family-friendly Seattle Center across the street and the McDonald's next door. Ditto the effect it has when pitted against Paul Allen's Experience Music Project/Hendrix Museum, a blobbish, Frank Gehry-designed eyesore with a music venue that serves $6 beers and blue cocktails. If Jimi were alive today, he'd play the Funhouse instead.

While the Funhouse has established itself as a punk-rock Shangri-La, the happy hour soundtrack is more varied, with Cypress Hill and Snoop getting equal time with head-banging fare. The bar's interior is dark and macabre, with faux spider webs lining the ceiling and a multitude of freaky clown portraits on the walls.

A quick editor's note: The reason why the Funhouse qualifies for this book and a similarly gritty place like El Corazon doesn't is that El Corazon is a music venue that happens to have a bar, whereas the Funhouse is a bar that happens to feature live music on most nights. That may be a nitpicky standard, but standards are the lifeblood of any great meritocracy. You're also not going to find any Irish pubs in this book, although if the Owl 'n Thistle lets itself go to seed over the next 10 years, it might make the second edition. And while Kelly's has an Irish name, it's about the furthest thing imaginable from an Irish pub.

Dive Bar Rating: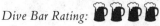

Pioneer Square Saloon

77 Yesler Way
Phone: 206-340-1234

There's a sign behind the bar at the Pioneer Square Saloon that says the following: "We like everybody: We like it when some people show up, and we like it when others leave." Stickers such as this are typically about as cerebral as Jeff Foxworthy, but this one really breaks the mold.

More classic saloon than tried and true dive, the Saloon is basically here because of its commitment to beer, as not serving hard liquor is a virtual bird-flip to the slew of freshly-minted, ultra-obnoxious, twenty-something drinkers which invades Pioneer Square Thursday through Saturday. Not that we have a problem with these folks: Amateurs in every city need a play-ground such as P-Square, where they can behave like complete idiots, engage in regrettable one-night stands, and test the limits of their tolerance. If it weren't for Pioneer Square, Belltown, Fremont, and Ballard would get exponentially more obnoxious, which would be a bad thing for the city's more accomplished, battle-tested drinkers who frequent those 'hoods.

The Saloon doesn't shun the rooks outright so much as it's set up to be unattractive to their ilk. Within a half-hour—tops—the bridge and tunneler's internal dialogue is likely to proceed as follows: "No red-headed sluts? No Jager-bombs? No Red Bull mixers? No shot girls? No deejay? No Ludacris? No techno? No cheesy cover band? No bachelorette parties? Where am I? Get me out of here!"

It's tough to recognize sometimes, but Pioneer Square has a rich creative tradition, with plenty of artists, writers, and musicians working or living in the historic neighborhood. Just as the area's bureaucrats, whose edifices of employment are concentrated nearby, deserve a place to gather and drink after work (that'd be the Collins Pub), so too does its bohemian set. Thank God, then, that the Saloon has managed to stick to its guns as one of the few adult watering holes amidst a sea of cheese.

Dive Bar Rating:

Sluggers

538 1st Ave. S.
Phone: 206-654-8070

Yep, you guessed it: This is a baseball bar. Even when it was called Sneakers, it was a baseball bar, even though baseball players generally wear cleats. There are framed photos of Mariners new and old on just about every available inch of wall, and enough television sets to ensure that every fan, no matter where he hails from, will get to watch his game.

The Mariners have been terrible lately, but their first 20 years, played in the hideous cement Kingdome, marked a sustained era of suckitude matched only by football's Detroit Lions. The M's were fucking awful; if they were within striking distance of .500 after Labor Day, it was tantamount to any another team making a late-season pennant bid. Granted, the franchise enjoyed a relatively sunny decade beginning in the mid-'90s, but for whatever reason, Sluggers will always remind me of the shit era, when Mickey Brantley, Bob Kearney, Todd Cruz, Cuffs Caudill, Rick Sweet or Richie Zisk were just as likely to occupy a post-game barstool as one of the handful of fans who stuck it out through the bottom of the ninth.

Sluggers is an extremely narrow bar that serves basic burgers and pub grub, with a space-saving two-top table scheme where compatriots face the wall of TVs rather than one another (there's an even narrower upper deck for couples seeking a more conversational drinking and dining experience). Recently, Congressman Jim McDermott was spotted quaffing beers in a blazer and bolo tie at Sluggers before the Robert Plant-Alison Krauss concert down the street. The show was at WaMu Theatre, so named for the failed thrift, and—irony of ironies—occurred just as Congress was taking up its massive financial industry bailout. To his credit McDermott made it back to D.C. on time to introduce a bill extending unemployment benefits the next morning. Play hard, work hard—Sluggers would expect nothing less of its Congressional customers.

Dive Bar Rating: 🍺🍺

Triangle Pub

The oldest of Seattle's three Triangles, this tiny, historic watering hole is all about baseball, a postage stamp facsimile of the sort of drinking scene that surrounds Wrigley Field before a Cub game. While you'll get a handful of all-day drinkers or pull-tab aces bellying up at the bar here, the bar typically fills up about an hour before the game and is deader than a doornail by the end of the first inning. (Quick question: Is a nail actually alive before it's hammered into a door hinge?)

The Triangle is not only one of Seattle's oldest bars, it's also one of its smallest. Hence, the majority of the pre-game crowd ends up drinking on a small patio out front. In actuality, this crowd, despite the best efforts of a stern doorman, pour onto the sidewalk. Occasionally a grill gets fired up for ballpark franks, although that's far from guaranteed, and quantity—22-oz. drafts of Pabst and 24-oz domestic tallboys—trumps quality at the bar by a good distance.

No matter how far the crowd spills into the public right away, you'll be in such close proximity to strangers that you can't help but befriend—or at least acknowledge and tolerate—the fat, sweaty guy who will unavoidably enter your personal space at some point. Maybe if you're lucky, you'll have seats near his at the game.

Dive Bar Rating:

The Siren Tavern

3403 4th Ave. S.
Phone: 206-223-9167

Located in a strip mall at the precipice of where SoDo's 4th Avenue strip fades into industrial oblivion, the Siren is a large, no-frills bar which stacks the regional dart publication, The Medallion, right alongside its *Weeklies* and *Strangers* at the front door. Its crowd is a mix between Mariner and Seahawk fans intent to wait out the post-game traffic over a pitcher, dart aficionados, workaday area employees who've recently punched out, and—at least on one of the nights I popped in—a crew of African-American bikers who favor super-fast sport bikes over hogs.

On a sleepy weeknight toward the end of the M's abysmal 2008 season, the hometown team is staging an unlikely comeback against the division-leading Angels on TV. The bar is relatively empty: There are a pair of husky women drinking and gossiping privately at one table, and a pair of young Asian guys getting clearly hustled by an animated older white guy at one of the pool tables. Conversing with the staff are a couple regulars: one a black guy drinking Coors and playing pull tabs, the other a skinny white guy guzzling screwdrivers. I've never understood people who drink screwdrivers at night, but to each his own.

While seemingly an unspectacular watering hole, the Siren does boast a hat-trick of divey hallmarks. For starters, they serve Schmidt by the can. Secondly, near the bar is a case of cheap jewelry for sale. Finally, there's a placard that reads: "Smile, you're on candid camera, for your safety and for ours." This isn't as foreboding as a paddy wagon parked out front or a bouncer with a metal detector, but it probably takes the bronze.

Dive Bar Rating: 🍺🍺🍺🍺

Targy's

600 W. Crockett
Phone: 206- 352-8885

Targy's is a virtually unmarked neighborhood bar that you don't just happen upon; you have to know exactly where it is. While Queen Anne Hill is relatively urban, Targy's is located atop its more anonymous western ridge, on an arterial used almost exclusively by neighborhood residents, and there isn't the sort of commercial clustering going on there like on Queen Anne Avenue, Upper Queen Anne's tony main drag.

Targy's used to serve only beer and wine and devoted a third of its space to ratty old couches, which gave it the feel of a fraternity party room. It also featured a notoriously prickly owner-bartender named Elmer Trestal, who was known for giving customers he'd never met before unprovoked verbal dressings down. But Trestal recently sold Targy's to a younger owner, who replaced the couches with unstained furniture, and added a small metal shelf of hard liquor, not to mention a handful of plasma screens for sports. While this results in the occasional youth invasion, Targy's is still very much a bar for nearby residents who want to enjoy a quiet beer or five – and its longest tenured bartender is missing an arm (he's still faster than 75 percent of the city's two-armed bartenders). While Targy's regulars don't carry AmEx gold cards, its crowd isn't as down and out as the Streamline's, if for no better reason as homeless people aren't likely to hoof it up the steep slope that connects Lower and Upper Queen Anne.

Much as I like Targy's, drinking there will forever feel a little like rooting for the Yankees, as they used to sponsor a perennially competitive softball team that used to be the chief rival of the team my father played on. I remember one game when Targy's whiner-in-chief, a tall dude with slicked back hair (only mega-tools put gel in their hair before sporting events), used to argue balls and strikes. In softball. There are certain things you don't do in life, and that's one of them.

Dive Bar Rating:

Streamline Tavern

Located a couple doors down from Ozzie's, the Streamline Tavern is as basic as taverns get. There's a large horseshoe bar, a couple TV sets, two or three small booths, and a pool table. It's one of the few taverns to offer Henry's on tap ($7.50 per pitcher) and cold six-packs to go. And if you need a glass of water between drafts, it'll be served neat, because there's no ice machine behind the bar.

When I stopped in for a beer one Saturday afternoon, an elderly Asian woman was tending bar, and an old white guy was nodding off at the bar, his nose nearly dipping into the beer before him. The bartender woke him up, but didn't kick him out. Surrounding the pair are half a dozen patrons, all well lubricated despite the fact that it was just a shade before five. A stubbly hustler walks in, trying to sell bootleg DVDs, but is shouted down by a noisy, vulgar blonde woman who informs him that she has a knife. He leaves, and her neighbors at the bar are astonished at her aggressive—check that, violent—tone. She informs them that the hustler in question harasses her constantly when he sees her on the streets; hence, her over-the-top posture was justified.

For a relatively affluent neighborhood, Lower Queen Anne has more than its fair share of transients and middle-class apartment dwellers, due in no small part to top-notch bus service and proximity to downtown. It comes as no surprise, then, when an emaciated, somewhat androgynous old woman wanders in, orders a beer, and takes a seat at one of the booths, with what are presumably her life's possessions parked in a metal cart next to her. After a few sips of beer, she gets up to go to the bathroom. By the time I get up to leave, roughly 20 minutes later, she still hasn't returned to her table.

Dive Bar Rating:

Mecca Cafe

526 Queen Anne Ave. N.
Phone: 206- 285-9728

Cameron Crowe's *Singles* is an amazingly annoying film, one of a handful to try and capture the spirit of the early '90s Seattle/Gen X grunge 'tude. While the music in the film is fantastic (save for Paul Westerberg's embarrassing "Dyslexic Heart"), Crowe reduces his ensemble characters to uptight, dissatisfied stereotypes, and Kyra Sedgwick's performance ranks among the worst in cinematic history.

But bad as Singles was, *Reality Bites* was worse. Whether the latter film was actually set in Seattle (it wasn't) is beside the point; as if the title could possibly leave a sliver of doubt in anyone's mind, it way-too-obviously tried to capitalize on the "I'm going to grow a goatee, not wash my hair, and chain smoke my way through what's I'm convinced is destined to be an incredibly shitty life, even though I come from a stable familial background, graduated from college, have no mouths to feed other than my own, and am in no threat of ending up on the streets" ethos of the day. It featured the actor most likely to get punched without provocation by me if we bumped into one another on the street, Ethan Hawke, as one of its leads, and another, Winona Ryder, who to this day sheds her (stolen) panties at the sight of any self-important, semi-talented pale white guy with a guitar on one shoulder and a chip on the other (see: Oberst, Conor). In other words, they were perfectly cast—if indeed the film's purpose was to twist a sword into the heart of a played-out era.

If either of these filmmakers had been genuinely interested in capturing the essence of the "life sucks" persona, they would have been better off camping out in the back booth of the Mecca with a Super 8 for a week. Behind any pose, there's authenticity—and the clientele at the Mecca is the real deal when it comes to drinking through the gloom. With 2/3 of its floor space devoted to a wee-hours diner that serves astonishingly good food based on what you'd expect from a greasy spoon, the cordoned-off bar area is so narrow that even Ryder would have to turn sideways to make it from one end to the other. What's more, the ceiling is high, homemade drawings and vulgar stickers cover the wall, the stereo is cranked to ear-splitting levels and typically tuned to Zeppelin or Black Sabbath, the crowd is a mix between blue-collar thirtysomethings and lonely, middle-aged men content to drown ever deeper in their sorrows. To top things off, the evening bartender is a hulking, highly competent pour man who values economy of language and movement.

The noontime tonic to such surliness is Jonesy, the bespectacled, strawberry blonde gentleman who opens the bar on most weekend mornings. Unlike his nighttime colleagues, Jonesy is interminably chipper, is willing to share his famous mac 'n cheese recipe with customers he likes, and makes a mean Bloody Mary. With Jonesy, at least, reality most definitely doesn't bite.

Dive Bar Rating: 🍺🍺🍺🍺

Jonathan Tuttle

Dome Stadium Tavern

214 Fourth Ave. S.
Phone: 206-624-7771

The fact that the domed stadium for which it is named was dynamited to smithereens to make way for a more modern, open-air structure doesn't seem to bother the Dome Stadium Tavern, described by one local scribe as "the dirtiest of the dirty and the seediest of the seedy." The Dome has done much to live up to this description in recent years, which have seen it busted for various drug-related improprieties, eventually resulting in a three-month, Liquor Control Borad-mandated license suspension that was lifted in February 2008 after many had left the hardscrabble tavern for dead.

The Dome is the sort of place that reinforces people's stereotypes of drunken Indians and unkempt winos who snatch purses and urinate in public. During happy hour, the crowd includes half a dozen severely inebriated Latino construction workers shouting to one another in Spanish. There are $2 pints of Busch on tap, and the jukebox is playing P-Funk as an androgynous Native American specimen whom the bartender addresses as "Alaska" walks in, sporting silver bracelets and flowing black hair. One of the construction workers, who's still wearing his orange reflective shirt, gets cut off by the take-no-shit female bartender, who's plastered Wonder Woman stickers behind the bar. Before he leaves, he opens his wallet to show her a photo of his daughter. Apparently, it's her niece; and quite obviously, he's fallen out of favor with his (ex?) wife's side of the family.

While the walls are painted earth tones, drinking beer here feels like drinking in the lobby of a fleabag hotel, of which there is a handful in nearby Chinatown. The cooler's inventory includes cans of energy drink, and there are bags of microwave popcorn and rice bowls available behind the bar. Two-dollar hot dogs are also advertised, but I see no evidence of their existence.

Dive Bar Rating:

Bernard's

Every night at Bernard's, sometime between 4:30 and 5, a waiter wanders downstairs, typically armed with a crockpot. In that crockpot, you might find cocktail weenies or maybe meatballs. And alongside that crockpot, you might find onion rings or taquitos. This food isn't to die for—not even close. But the price—free—couldn't be more right.

Located beneath the Hotel Seattle, Bernard's is one of the last quaint, dowdy hotel bars around in the city, the sort of place where lawyers, cops, journalists, and politicians are apt to meet to discuss private matters, which makes for peerless eavesdropping. That said, if I wanted to put a hit out on somebody, this is where I'd go, as it would simply be a matter of sequestering myself at a back table with an underworld associate to avoid being heard. It'd also be the bar I'd seek temporary refuge in if there was an attack on American soil, if a plane flew into the Columbia Tower Club, if a sequel to the WTO riots broke out in the streets, or if a tsunami was predicted to engulf downtown Seattle's lowlands. Bernard's might be a lonely, unspectacular watering hole, but if nothing else, it feels safe.

Basement bars are a great place to hide out from the world—not to mention the weather, if it sucks, as it often does in Seattle. Here, you can create your own alternate reality. Underground, you can pretend to be anyone you want, anywhere in the world.

Dive Bar Rating:

Shorty's Coney Island

2222 Second Ave.
Phone: 206-441-5449

For as long as Belltown has been *Belltown*, Shorty's has run against the neighborhood's nouveau-riche grain by casting its lot with tube steaks and canned beer, the sum of which can be covered with whatever soiled greenbacks you've got scrunched in the side pocket of your favorite pair of jeans from the prior night's debauchery. Shorty's is also the best place in the city for folks with restless fingers, as very inch of spare space is devoted to arcade games or pinball machines—many vintage. Even the sit-down tables double as some sort of coin-consuming amusement.

There's an addictive quality to Shorty's. As with any good, sleazy, peep show theater, even the most glorious of summer days aren't enough to dissuade Shorty's pinball wizards from getting their daily (daylong?) fix. Before his band plays three-show runs at the nearby Croc, Built to Spill frontman Doug Martsch can reliably be found silently relieving his pockets of spare change, singularly focused on whatever video realm lurks on the screen before him. Provided they've got a beer perched somewhere near them, this is as close as many people are willing to come to drinking alone.

Shorty's also happens to sit on downtown Seattle's most dynamic block of entertainment. On one corner is Mama's Mexican Kitchen, a charmingly kitschy restaurant that holds Elvis Presley in high esteem. On the other is the legendary Crocodile Café, recently reopened after being hung up in a scary state of proprietary limbo. In between is the cheap, delicious Noodle Ranch, the dark, hip Lava Lounge, and Tula's, one of the few places around town to catch live jazz on a walk-in basis. Then, smack in the middle, there's Shorty's and its merry band of gamers, oblivious to their surroundings.

Dive Bar Rating: 🍺🍺🍺

Nite Lite

1926 2nd Ave.
Phone: 206- 448-4852

The Nite Lite is not only the best dive bar in downtown Seattle, it's downtown Seattle's best bar, period (bear in mind this opinion comes from the author of a book about dive bars). It's kind of the perfect combination of everything: kitsch, authenticity, crustiness, greasiness, affordability, inebriation, conversation, professionalism, mischievousness, friendliness, youth, creativity, vigor, honor, loyalty—all of these qualities can be found at the Nite Lite.

Drinking at the Nite Lite, with its fondness for formica, peculiar furniture, and bright little lights, is like drinking in Pee-Wee's Playhouse. The crowd is every bit as colorful as the décor; one recent happy hour featured an ex-Mormon with a pitcher all her own, telling a story about how she went to Vegas for a Springsteen concert but declined to rent a room for the night, instead walking the streets and gambling until her flight out the next morning—a strategy that really only works (brilliantly) in Sin City. While nights when the Showbox or Moore is hosting a hot show often result in a cadre of hip, young patrons, things rarely boil into anything bad.

Upon entry, customers will find a handful of tables and television sets, a jukebox, and the bar, which is inevitably staffed by a sweet old pro you're tempted to refer to as Aunt Martha, even if her name's not Martha. A couple steps beneath the bar is a living room set's worth of cushy furniture. (Beware the dart boards, however.) On the rare occasions when these spaces get too stuffed, an employee will unlock a spacious dining room near the latrines, where surplus tables can be commandeered.

The Nite Lite has $2 pints of Pabst on tap at all hours, and accepts only cash. If they're fresh out of your liquor of choice—as happened to me after a Lucinda Williams show when they were out of Old Overholt and I had to settle for SoCo—you can be sure that whatever you're forced to quaff instead will be poured generously, to put it mildly. They've got food at the Nite Lite, but consider the following anecdote, based on actual events, before heading there on an empty stomach:

A guy walks into the Nite Lite and orders a sandwich that includes bacon as a primary ingredient. Upon being informed that the bar is out of bacon, he asks if he can substitute mushrooms. "Come on," snaps the bartender, "this is the Nite Lite"—and that's the extent of her reply. So which is it: no mushrooms or no substitutions? It really shouldn't matter; the message is clear enough as is.

Dive Bar Rating:

Fortune Sports Bar

664 S. King St.
Phone: 206-223-0123

A lower-key cousin to Lake City's crack-a-lackin' Rose Garden, Fortune Sports Bar caters mainly to older dudes who are either down on their luck, down on their supply, or down to get down with the happy hour bartender, a lovely young Asian woman in a short denim skirt who is flirtatious to the point where you feel as though a complimentary HJ might be in the offing. But don't let this fool you; when it comes to enforcing Fortune's "no bagpack after 8 p.m." rule, homegirl can hold the line. That rule—bagpack equals backpack—is one of two designed to deter homeless freeloaders from sidling up to the bar, the other being a ban on "overnight tabs" (what is this, Cheers?) that the bar chalks up to the current "economic downfall."

While some regulars flock for the chicken gizzards and fish balls, others speak in tongues, such as a guy who announced he'd had five back surgeries before announcing several other things we couldn't make heads or tails of. Upon entering this sparsely-decorated Chinatown establishment, patrons will pass two pool tables before encountering the bar, which boasts a pair of bizarre, white liquor cases which look as though they've been pilfered from *A Clockwork Orange's* milk bar. The more drinks you order, the stiffer those drinks will get. And if you order beer, the bartender will try—repeatedly—to cajole you into ordering a shot, punctuating her pleas with a sassy "woo-hoo!" (If you decline to order actual shots of liquor, she'll fill a shot glass with peanuts.)

Half of Fortune's space is devoted to a high-celinged club area, with a staging area for karaoke or live music (the Tittleholders—not Titleholders, Tittleholders—was one recent act) and a small, elevated VIP area consisting only of a sectional couch. While the women's bathroom is surprisingly clean, the men's latrine features spackled walls and crumbling tiles.

Like the Rose Garden, Fortune is the sort of place that can be filled with customers one minute, then empty for the next five, then filled back up again five minutes later. We'll venture to guess this has something to do with the deep conversations occurring on the sidewalk out front, as well as the patrons who stroll in and out of a mysterious "Employee Only" area with impunity.

Dive Bar Rating: 🍺🍺🍺🍺🍺

Kerri Harrop

Bush Garden

614 Maynard Ave. S.
Phone: 206-682-6830

Not to be confused with the similarly-named African theme park in Florida, Seattle's Bush Garden is nevertheless a jungle of drunken song, perhaps the most iconic karaoke venue in the entire city.

I can't prove the staff is perennially shitfaced here—I've never been an eyewitness to on-the-job imbibing—but if they aren't, I want to know their secret. The cocktail waitress is barfly-hooker friendly, and the KJ slurs his words to the point where he needs a translator when he's calling singers to the stage. And when we say stage, we don't mean a mere area for soloists to launch into "Total Eclipse of the Heart"—we mean a proper stage, like you'd find in a nightclub. While Bush Garden frequently attracts a Petri dish of Caucasian hipster interlopers, it remains a Chinatown bar, and Asian folk take their karaoke seriously—to the point where nothing less than a proper stage will do.

While Bush Garden has been around since the '50s, its jagged rock exterior belongs in a '70s Scorsese film. This nostalgic aesthetic is commonplace in Chinatown, home to Seattle's most famous mass murder, the Wah Mee Massacre, in which 14 people were gunned down at one of the West Coast's most popular, albeit illegal (cops turned a blind eye at the time), underground gambling parlors in 1983. Chinatown is not considered a dangerous neighborhood, but it retains a smelly, seedy, hyper-urban, trip-back-in-time-to-a-faraway-metropolis allure that no other neighborhood in the city can hold a candle to. When dyed-in-the-wool Seattleites get bored with the rest of the city, Chinatown is their escape.

Dive Bar Rating:

Dynasty Room

714 S. King St
Phone: 206-682-4900

The lounge area of the 74-year-old Four Seas restaurant will never favor of-the-moment indie rock on its jukebox, nor will it have an extensive variety of revolving Northwest microbrews on tap. It will never stage art installations with superhot DJs providing mood music. It will never feature jalapeno poppers on its appetizer menu, nor will it ever refer to an appetizer as an "appeteaser." The Dynasty Room is, simply, a dimly-lit International District lounge that serves stiff cocktails, Tsing Tao beer, and scrumptious chive won-tons.

My friend Shawn once aptly compared the Dynasty Room to the Bat Cave; the sort of place where Batman would meet with Gotham City's political elite to figure out how to deal with an emergent criminal tidal wave. It's also something of a political hangout, mainly by virtue of the fact that Seattle City Councilmember Richard McIver used to come here religiously at the stroke of five for Johnny Walker-soaked "office hours"—until one such confab resulted in his arrest on domestic violence charges and the subsequent derailing of his career. (McIver was eventually cleared of any criminal wrongdoing after his wife, who occasionally joined him at the bar, refused to testify.)

The bar's top shelf, which includes relatively pedestrian liquors like Patron and Hennessy, is labeled as "Dynasty Room's Private Reserve." There's a broken cigarette machine positioned next to a broken Triv Whiz against one of the walls, which features an old-school Henry Weinhard's pennant. By days, the television sets are usually tuned to soap operas, and the afternoon bartender is a pushy old woman who scowls— only half-jokingly—at anyone who considers it ill form to drink more than two beers with their dim sum.

Dive Bar Rating: 🍺🍺

EAST-CENTRAL SEATTLE

EASTLAKE
CAPITOL HILL
CENTRAL DISTRICT
MADISON PARK

The Seattle Eagle

314 E. Pike St.
Phone: 206-621-7591

Unmarked façade near cluttered urban intersection: check. Dark, narrow entryway leading to dark, narrow bar area: check. Nonstop guy-on-guy porn projected on large screen near bar: check. Buff, shirtless bartender: check. Shirtless patrons: check. Mysterious, caged balcony where unspeakable acts are said to occur: check. General hostility directed toward women patrons: check. Random, unsolicited ass-grabbing of male patrons: check.

Welcome to the Seattle Eagle, a dark, seedy hole-in-the-wall that puts the "stereo" in "stereotypical gay bar." Not that there's anything wrong with that; some gay bars are very welcoming and comfortable environments for straight people and women, some aren't. The Eagle is of the latter variety, and there are like-minded Eagles—not to be confused with the august fraternal organization of the same name—in many major cities.

With a small neon beer sign in a small window serving as the lone signifier of its very existence, from the outside, the Eagle looks like it could just as easily be the storeroom for neighboring Benson's Grocery, a mini-mart that serves a largely transient population. Last I visited the Eagle, it was Bareback Thursday, where customers get a dollar knocked off their drinks if they take their shirts off. This doesn't result in cheap drinks, however—my bourbon-soda set me back a pretty ridiculous $7.50. It was, however, stiff, and the bear-licious bartender was super sweet—even to the ladies. Projected on a screen overhead was a gay porno set in the great outdoors, which led to a discussion about another outdoorsy film involving a bunch of hot young Australian dudes.

The best Eagle story I've heard is from a lesbian named Debbie. One night, she witnessed a guy sucking another guy off on the balcony while watching porn. When asked by a bystander if she liked the flick, she responded, "When in Rome." This guy then launched into a tirade about how gay cock was just like straight cock, to which Debbie replied that she was gay. He then said curtly, "Lesbian night is Wednesday," and stormed off.

Dive Bar Rating: 🍺🍺🍺🍺

GAY DIVES

THE CRESCENT

MADISON PUB

CHANGES

C.C. ATTLE'S

SEATTLE EAGLE

The Crescent

Located within a short walk of the Eagle on Capitol Hill, the Crescent is a spectacularly friendly, come-one-come-all, gay karaoke bar whose crowd probably runs at least a third straight on any given night. But while anyone can hang out and have a great time at the Crescent, the karaoke stage isn't for everyone. Here, amateurs and those who need the security blanket of singing with friends need not apply, as tone deafness and duets are frowned upon.

They have karaoke every night at the Crescent, and the mix of singers is a pretty evenly split between show tune queens, folkie dykes, and androgynous hipsters who like to rock. At just about any other karaoke bar in the city, I'd argue for a ban on deejays taking the mikes themselves, but not here; the Crescent's KJ's can fucking sing. Plus they have names like DJ Johnny Cockring, which is awesome. Song choices are all over the map, from Sinatra to Haggard, Satchmo to Aretha. Singers aren't afraid to step way outside their comfort zones; probably my favorite Crescent performance was when a skinny black skater got up to sing "Hollywood Nights" by Bob Seger—and nailed it.

The karaoke stage sits in a gulch next to the bar, which is right by the entrance. There are also a handful of tables on a slightly elevated area near the rear of the room. Drinks aren't dirt cheap, but aren't unfairly priced either; and the bartenders, who are as varied in looks and predilections as the crowd, pour with regard to maximum impact. It is virtually impossible to think of two more diametrically opposed gay bars than the Eagle and the Crescent. I'll take the Crescent any day of the week, but then, I prefer the hole to the pole. To each his own.

Dive Bar Rating:

Bill's Off Broadway

725 E. Pine St.
Phone: 206-323-7200

In a neighborhood known for its aggressive eccentricity, Bill's Off Broadway is welcome tonic. With its plain wooden interior, Bill's is the sort of low-key pizza and beer bar you can find just about anywhere—which is why it's so strange to find it on Capitol Hill.

I walked into Bill's to meet a friend at 6:30 on a Wednesday last summer. I took a seat at the bar, which is separated from a slew of tables by a partition and a couple downward steps. The place was empty, to the point where I wondered if I'd inadvertently walked in on a private party that had yet to begin. But then I remembered that Capitol Hill, more than any other neighborhood in town, keeps hours more akin to Manhattan than Seattle.

I ordered a cheap pint of Pabst, something I regretted slightly after seeing a couple Busch tallboys in an ice bin built into the bar (I'm convinced that Busch will eventually be the new Pabst, in spite of its Anheuser-Busch roots). The wooden bar area is decorated sparsely; indoor plants that look like they haven't been watered in awhile are what pass for an aesthetic flourish. A few sips into my Pabst, a manager invites me to sample from a platter of fresh smoked salmon, giving the place the feel of a laid-back house party as more customers start to slowly file in.

I've had pizza at Bill's on several occasions, and it's been hit-or-miss. But when what most bars of this ilk offer in the way of pizza is glorified Tombstone, the mere fact that Bill's makes its own pies from scratch is a pretty significant upgrade. What I can say is that on my last visit there, the pepperoni and mushroom pie my drinking companion and I wolfed down was scrumptious, even if it was a bit overpriced. Just when I start to think I prefer fried chicken with my beer, pizza brings me back.

Dive Bar Rating:

Eastlake Zoo Tavern

2301 Eastlake Ave. E.
Phone: 206-329-3277

Anybody who thinks hunters and hippies can't harmoniously coexist needs to pay a visit to the Zoo. With its virtually windowless exterior and beastly name, the Zoo could easily be mistaken for a clandestine gay bar back when gay bars were considered taboo. But inside, the setup's pretty straight: pool tables, darts, shuffleboard, peanuts, beer, taxidermy mounted on the walls, sports on TV, and the Stones on the speakers. In short, the Zoo is a dude den par excellence, and has been, unwaveringly, for more than 30 years, even as the neighborhood around it has taken an intensely highfalutin turn (Bogey's and Fat Albert's, R.I.P.).

The Zoo has long been a co-op whose employees have an ownership stake. Recently, this structure was threatened by Seattle's changing liquor landscape. The Zoo refuses to serve anything stronger than red wine, and after a temporary dip in business, has rebounded, packing back on the pounds of patronage. "I think you can still make money not serving hard alcohol," says Zoo manager Howard Brown. "People come in to play games and socialize. There's something to be said about places where people are just drinking wine or beer. It's more leisurely."

This is what's endeared Paul Zemann to places like the Zoo. By day, Zemann works for King County as a drug and alcohol specialist. By night, he kicks back and sips beer at taverns countywide—taverns strictly defined in Washington State as venues that serve only beer and wine. "My passion for taverns is not the alcohol," says Zemann, a mustachioed walrus of a man who favors all-denim outfits. "It's the 'third place' principle. At a restaurant, you've got your family, but you come to the tavern and you're with the crowd. People aren't here slamming them down. Beer and wine, the point is not to get drunk, it's to drink socially and have a conversation."

The novelist Tom Robbins, who resides near Seattle, shares Zemann's philosophy. "You can discuss art and politics for hours on end over pitchers of beer and remain relatively coherent; there's even a time early on when you're more eloquent than normal. But most people can't drink a lot of whiskey and remain conversant in any sort of entertaining and intellectually stimulating sort of way."

Dive Bar Rating:

Comet Tavern

922 E. Pike St.
Phone: 206-322-9272

The Comet was once one of the city's most bona fide dives, all piss odors, cigarette smoke, cheap beer, and disheveled patrons. Puke rimming the toilet? Yep. Regulars nodding off well before closing time? Naturally. If grunge were a tavern, it would have been the Comet. The place was jolly old cesspool of unadulterated filth—in a good way.

A few years ago, the Comet's ownership changed hands. To the new proprietors' credit, they didn't dick with the interior; it still feels as lived-in as ever—although it looks as though somebody actually takes a rag to the bar every once in awhile now. But they broke with tradition by serving hard booze and booking live music. These changes have attracted a hipper, younger clientele. The Comet is now more accessible and potentially sustainable, but at what cost?

On the one hand, the regulars haven't been scared off entirely, especially during the day. And the Comet's booker, a woman known as Mama Casserole, has a really keen ear for up-and-coming rock acts. But at times, the Comet unwittingly serves as a clubhouse for the worst Capitol Hill has to offer. I'm not talking about hardened criminals or people looking to start shit, I'm talking about purposefully emaciated, ironically tattooed, skinny jeans-wearing, trust-fund drawing, coke-snorting, faux impoverished, ultra-cynical Nightlife Nazis who make the Pike-Pine corridor virtually unbearable for people who don't subscribe to their signature look and 'tude. Specifically, I'm talking about the guy with the pierced eyebrows, manscara, pageboy hat, and v-neck t-shirt who pretended to not know which friend's couch he was going to crash on that night. Dude, I saw the purebred puppy in your designer backpack. You're crashing on the couch in the $500,000 condo your parents just bought you, brother. Give it up.

Dive Bar Rating: 🍺🍺🍺🍺🍺

Charlie's on Broadway

217 Broadway Ave. E.
Phone: 206-323-2535

I don't like to drink at Applebee's, but sometimes I like to drink at bars that feel like Applebee's. The lure is essentially a two-fisted chug of critical attributes: anonymity and efficiency. When there's no scene, and you're not at a place to see and be seen, you can get right down to the business of drinking. Usually when I'm drinking alone, it's because I have some post-meal time to kill before I have to meet someone for a rock show later on. This was precisely my predicament last I paid a visit to Charlie's on Broadway.

At Charlie's there's absolutely no governing interior design principle. Look no further than the bicycle hanging from the roof with a mannequin in a candy-striped vest piloting the handlebars for proof of this. Not that I care; I'm here to consume three rounds of what Charlie's bartender refers to as "a meal"—shot of tequila, with beer and water backs—within the course of an hour. Deplete the liver; then irrigate—high risk, high reward, stern buzz.

When I sit down at the right-hand corner of the bar, there is but one other patron to my left, an old white guy drinking red wine. He's soon joined by an old black guy who orders Scotch. These two old guys obviously know each other, and quickly ease into a rapport centered on local sports. Beyond the bar, a couple guys are shooting pool. In between racks, they keep plugging really good songs by really good artists—the Who, Al Green, Zeppelin—into the jukebox.

Before long, a full-figured young woman named Tracy takes a seat between me and the old guys. The bartender, who's clad in a pressed white dress shirt and black slacks, asks her what she's up to. She says she's chosen to go to Charlie's because she didn't want to "get pretty" in order to go someplace else. If that isn't a testament to Charlie's value here on earth, I don't know what is.

Dive Bar Rating:

Red Onion Tavern

4210 E. Madison St.
Phone: 206-323-1611

Of all the neighborhoods to boast two century-old taverns, hyper-yuppified Madison Park might be the unlikeliest. But here they are, down by the lakeshore: the Attic and the Red Onion, places where our dads' dads joyously tilted back schooners while in their drinking prime.

While the Attic and its scrumptious pub fare is the more popular diamond, the Onion is the rough. Unlike the Attic, the Onion is more liquid-centric—the pizza on the menu is edible but more for show. While it's no dump, the Onion has a lived-in, rumpled feel; with a fireplace on one wall, the bar's most frequent utility is as a fishing cabin catch-drain for the Attic's oft-packed ski-lodge singles scene down the street.

It was in that catch-drain where I found myself on a Wednesday after lunch, nursing a pint of Rainier and reading next to a silver, chardonnay-sipping fox in Chanel suspenders. Slurring her speech by 2 in the afternoon, this woman asked me if I thought the bartender was a good-looking man. Before I could respond in the affirmative, the bartender reprimanded her for asking what he considered to be an inappropriate question.

The silver fox spent the next several minutes leaving several messages on several doctors' answering machines, seeking some sort of prescription for a sore throat. Meanwhile, the bartender pointed out a newspaper item where some woman who'd just purchased a meat smoker found an amputated human leg beneath the hood. The name of the smoker's owner was Peg.

Dive Bar Rating:

Madison Pub

1315 E. Madison
Phone: 206-325-6537

The Madison Pub is the least-gay gay bar in Seattle, and quite possibly in the history of man-on-mankind. Sure, there's a rainbow flag flying proudly out front and the crowd is all dudes, but other than that, this ultra-friendly watering hole is virtually indistinguishable from any straight neighborhood bar in the city, and proof that not all gay bars are squarely focused on cruising (not that you can't get action here, but you can get action waiting to renew your driver's license given the right set of circumstances).

The pub has no food—unless you count peanuts—and all the television sets are tuned to sports. (Come to think of it, aren't most sports bars populated almost exclusively by men?) There's a large, comfortable pool room, and even a separate room for darts. The guys range in age from 30 to 60, are dressed very casually, and seem more likely to bro-down with a cavalcade of shots than to lay the groundwork for a late-night bone-crushing session. While it's not packed in the middle of the week, my friend Jonathan says it's not uncommon to find a line out the door on weekends, as there aren't enough bar's like it that cater to gay men of a certain age.

What differentiates the Madison Pub from Changes, other than the fact that it's far bigger, is the music. At Changes, it's a steady diet of queeny remixes and electronica; at the Madison Pub, it's a steady diet of rock and roll served with a splash of R&B. Simply put, it's straight-friendly to the point where the average heterosexual gent wouldn't think twice about heading back in for a beer on his own volition, unaccompanied by his gay male or straight female buddyguards.

Dive Bar Rating:

Thompson's Point of View

2308 E. Union St.
Phone: 206-329-2512

Man, what a name. But it sure is sad that Thompson's has to have an offensive tackle with a metal-detecting wand patting down customers at 7 p.m. on a Tuesday. If the Central District has a notorious corner, 23rd & Union is it, although what passes for "notorious" in Seattle would make a Chicagoan laugh his fanny off.

The CD is, without question, Seattle's most historically important black neighborhood, the birthplace of Seattle's Panther Party and home to the NAACP, Mt. Zion Baptist Church, and virtually every important civil rights institution and movement the city has witnessed. But recent history has seen a large influx of upper middle class whites in the CD, as many blacks have cashed in on skyrocketing (pre-recession) home prices and moved to areas like South King County, replicating a now-familiar trend where certain city's most diverse neighborhoods are no longer actually located within the city limits (see: San Francisco, Calif.).

Although its extinction predates the whitening of the Central District at large by decades, Seattle's most tragic nightlife casualty was the dissolution of the live music district around 23rd and Jackson. Now the only reminder —and it's an incredibly lame one—of that marvelously freewheeling scene is a Starbucks with trumpet players painted on the wall. But while you won't find live jazz at Thompson's Point of View, the restaurant-lounge is to the CD's black community as Kelly's is to Belltown's transient community: the last vestige of what was before Seattle polished its molars for the world to see. There is a mural on the establishment's western wall that features paintings of prominent local African-Americans like Edwin Pratt. The happy hour crowd consists exclusively of middle-aged black folks, one of whom bemoans the fact that you can't buy setups (full bottle of liquor, along with the mix-er of your choice) in Washington, as you can in other states. Another wonders, at the top of his lungs, why anyone in their right mind would ever order a red beer.

"If I want tomato juice, I'll order a tomato juice," he says. "If I want beer, I'll order a beer."

Up at the bar, the conversation between two older black men is centered on their concern for the future of young black people, the sort of conversation you'd expect to hear at an Urban League stakeholders' summit. It's a conversation that is unlikely to end until the doorman at Thompson's no longer has to whip out his wand before letting people in.

Dive Bar Rating: 🍺🍺🍺🍺

Canterbury Ale & Eats

534 15th Ave. E.
Phone: 206-322-3130

I'm sitting at the Canterbury, a cavernous, Olde English dive located on the mellower of Capitol Hill's two main north-south strolls, drinking whiskey with a buddy who's just kicked a cute girl to the curb because she didn't like soup. Soup! Who doesn't like soup? I mean, you can dislike a certain kind of soup. I hate cheddar-broccoli soup, for instance, and am a fairly finicky eater in general. But man, do I love split pea and ham. Soup can contain about as many ingredients as there are types of food; if you're going to issue such a blanket dismissal, you mustn't like to eat, period.

There were other reasons why things didn't work out between this pair. She didn't like reggae either, which actually would have been acceptable were it not for the following caveat: she liked dancehall. Dancehall is a subset of reggae; not at least respecting the progenitor is like saying you're a big fan of Jesus Christ but think his dad is sort of a deadbeat, too consumed with his job to spend time with his only son. It's like saying you're crazy about Mick Jagger's solo albums but think the Stones really blow. Maybe she was just trying too hard to impress a guy who's ridiculously well-versed in music (my buddy writes about music for a living). But in fact, she achieved the exact opposite objective.

Anyway, back to the Canterbury: On the south end of the establishment is a large game room with no table service. In the middle is the dark bar portion, where you'll want to order drinks if you're either sitting in the bar or gaming in the game room. When my pal and I walked in, we ordered at the bar, and then set about looking for a pair of nearby seats. There were none, and so we commandeered the last table in the Canterbury's parlor, a bright space with a fireplace that's good for reading and picking up Helen Mirren.

As soon as our bottoms hit the chair, we were confronted

by a waitress, who looked at us in horror, pointed at a sign, and said, "Guys! If you want to order drinks at the bar, go to the game room." We apologized, told her she could charge us a sitting fee if she felt so inclined, and informed her that we were expecting two more companions and would make it worth her while by the time we left. She stammered off, but soon returned to take our next drink order. Two hours and a hundred-dollar tab later, her frown had turned upside down. I wonder if she hates soup too.

Dive Bar Rating:

Jonathan Tuttle

C.C. Attle's

1501 E. Madison
Phone: 206-323-4017

CC Attle's has multiple personalities. Let's start with the fact that while the bar at large is known as CC's, one of its rooms is called the Men's Room, and the patio is formally known as the Veranda Room. Its crowd tends to be older and beefier than other gay bars, probably residual from when CC's hosts its bear night every first Saturday of each month, which finds the bar smolderingly cramped with very hairy men and the dudes who adore them.

I visited CC's with a group of guys that included Alonzo, a gay "Mexi-bear" who's none too fond of either that term or gay bars in general. When we walked in, some stock techno was blasting on the stereo, and the TVs were filled with a never-ending loop of still photos featuring men with enormous or unusual (i.e., pierced) cocks.

"This music, these pictures—come on!" scoffed Alonzo, as a cook rang the order up bell for a plate of onion rings. "It's like Cockapalooza up there."

Not that a bartender at a gay bar owes a couple dudes who don't like looking at naked guys anything, but if he did, he more than atoned while pouring us a round of six "Gayhounds"—grapefruit juice with Ruby Red vodka. As if his first five pours weren't stiff enough, when he got around to pouring Alonzo's drink, the plastic spigot on the vodka bottle fell off, meaning Alonzo got a tumbler filled with nothing but grapefruit-flavored vodka.

In CC's main room, aside from the omnipresent Cockapalooza reel, is an enormous, hilariously kitschy sailor statue, with shoulders so ripped they're more reminiscent of clamshells than muscles. This is also where, unannounced, a goateed patron came up to me unannounced and grabbed a handful of my ass, complimenting me on having a "great booty." What else could I do but thank him? If only straight women were so forward in their advances.

Dive Bar Rating: 🍺🍺

SOUTH SEATTLE

GEORGETOWN
SOUTH PARK
BEACON HILL
RAINIER VALLEY

Copper Door Tavern

SOUTH SEATTLE * GEORGETOWN

SEATTLE'S BEST DIVE BARS

I think I'm on relatively safe terrain when I pledge to encode the following as something that automatically qualifies a bar as a dive: When the lunch crowd includes a wild-eyed, wheelchair-bound guy drinking straight rum and yelling "aargh!" without provocation, that's a fucking dive bar. Ooh, and one more: Any place that serves Schmidt Ice—or Schmidt, period—is most definitely a dive bar. With that, I proudly induct into the fold the Copper Door, where both of these conditions apply.

They have food at the Copper Door, but it's something of a charade. People come here during the day to drink. Many of the black rubber barstools are patched up by duct tape, and most of them are full of lushes by the middle of the day on a Wednesday. There's a mellow old-timer who appears to be downing a can of Schmidt Ice every five minutes, and a hyper middle-aged guy guzzling pitcher after pitcher without any help. After a few minutes, a couple sooty-looking gentlemen who appear to have just gotten off work show up and order a shot and a beer apiece (the Copper Door is surrounded by industrial businesses where graveyard and swing shifts are prevalent). The drinkers here don't screw around; every ounce of pain incurred during the work day—or perhaps over the course of two tours in 'Nam—is going to be matched in consumption at the bar.

At night, an immensely friendly Asian woman that everyone calls Mrs. Wu—or something along those lines —presides over the bar. What there is of the sparse crowd is younger than the daytime lot, and one of these guys seems to be using the Copper Door to post up in between drug runs. Unsolicited, a hippie-looking dude shares his life philosophy with us: "All you need is to smoke a joint." Yes, sir.

Dive Bar Rating: 🍺🍺🍺🍺

Annex Tavern

10325 E. Marginal Way
Phone: 206-763-7207

Everybody knows every word to every song at the Annex, a karaoke and R&B hotbed located in an industrial riverside no-man's land just south of the Seattle city limit on East Marginal Way. While ruffians are prone to drop in from time to time, the Annex is the bar Lake City's Rose Garden could be if it had any class.

Based on its location near the south end of Boeing Field, the Annex should be a bar where a bunch of machinists come to obliterate the daily grind with whiskey and bitch about their jobs. That assuredly happens here from time to time, but it's the exception to the rule. The Annex's crowd, especially for weekend karaoke, is mostly middle-aged black people.

A pebble's skip from the Duwamish with no residential structures for miles, the Annex benefits from about zero foot traffic. It's not the sort of bar you stumble in to, but that doesn't mean it fails to attract its fair share of newcomers—even from out of town. To wit, we encountered Harold, a good-looking African-American guy in town on business from Atlanta. Tired of unwinding at the sterile, monotonous hotel bars near Sea-Tac Airport, Harold was steered north to the Annex on a recommendation from a friend. Here, he joined a hodgepodge of characters that included a couple younger brothers, a black chick wearing a bandana and sunglasses who peppered the jukebox with requests, an older Russian guy slouched over the bar, and a manic Caucasian bartender with a Hawaiian print shirt.

Whereas at the Rose Garden, such a mix might lead to a scrum, at the Annex, a live and let live vibe prevails. Look no further than the strength of Harold's drink and the width of his smile for proof of that.

Dive Bar Rating:

The Beacon Pub

His name is Earl. He's skinny, wears·sunglasses at night, has a wide gap in the middle of his upper row of teeth, and wears a stocking cap, even during summertime. He looks like Flava Flave, and enjoys chatting up the ladies. But he's not the sort of aspiring Lothario who shuns the conversation of men in order to keep his mouth on the prize. Earl is from Louisiana and a friend to all, a devotee to Beacon Hill's lone true watering hole, the Beacon Pub.

Home to the city's largest concentration of single-family homes containing Asian-Americans, Beacon Hill towers high above the Rainier Valley to the east, Georgetown to the west, and downtown to the northwest. Mainly a bedroom community, Beacon Hill is decidedly unhip; a friend of mine who lives there jokingly refers to it as "Georgetown Heights" in an effort to cool up her street address.

While it plays host to the occasional brandished firearm, the Beacon Pub's reputation far outstrips its reality. It's a little grimy, but not a lot grimy, toeing the line between friendly neighborhood alehouse and well-worn dive. But still, judging from how difficult it is to get a cab to pick you up at the Beacon, you'd think the place was located in the Seventh Circle of Hell. I suspect all the hullabaloo surrounding the Beacon is due to good old-fashioned racism; the bar is frequented by mostly black people, while the Asian-Americans and young whites who've recently migrated to the neighborhood on account of affordability generally shy away. Therefore, the latter two groups have developed an overblown notion of what goes on behind the Beacon's supposedly ferocious four walls.

Sure, the Beacon gets a little unruly at times—especially back by the pool table—and has random salad spinners and George Foreman Grills above the bar. But there are manifold plays at respectability. For one, the bartenders are young, hip, cute, and usually female. Secondly, a pint of microbrew costs $4 here, which is beyond the budget of your average poverty line drunk. That sort of exorbitant pricing kind of sucks for everyone—at least there are Rainier tallboys in the cold case.

Dive Bar Rating:

Marco Polo Bar & Grill

5613 4th Ave. S.
Phone: 206-762-3964

Unlike its Middle American counterparts, Seattle is not a city that teems with great fried chicken 'n beer joints. Which is too bad, because if there were more bars like the Marco Polo, you'd have the makings of a great debate: Which is better with beer, fried chicken or pizza?

The first thing you notice about the Marco Polo is not its chicken or beer, however, but the gorgeous, neon green, Route 66-era sign out front, the illuminated "Saloon" melting into an arrow that points you into the door. Once inside, you'll find a schizophrenic interior – part bingo hall, part fireside-turtleneck wine bar. The crowd, however, is decidedly working class. There are a lot of TVs, but at least half of them are tuned to a peculiar satellite trivia game that, judging from the craned necks of many patrons, seems to have developed quite a following. Rounding out the scene are pull tabs, pool tables, and the occasional karaoke night.

A couple other peculiarities here: the kitchen churns out sensational pepperoni grinders and chili-cheese fries, and the bar offers free Dixie Cups of ice cream to every diner. Chicken, beer, grinders, chili-cheese fries, and ice cream in a bingo hall setting—where are we, anyway, Cedar Rapids?

Dive Bar Rating:

Wildwood Tavern

7631 Rainier Ave. S.
Phone: 206-722-9444

On a sunny midweek afternoon, the Wildwood Tavern's bartender flips the TV from an old action movie to baseball, and a Filipino guy comes in and orders a bottle of Bud—to go—joined shortly thereafter by an elderly white guy named Dick, who plops down in front of a $1.50 schooner of Busch. In the corner is a guy collecting quarters from one of the bar's arcade games. Dick asks him how old he is. He replies that he's 58, and is looking forward to the time when he can sit around all day and drink beer like Dick.

At night, half-a-dozen Latino gentlemen of various ages drink and carry on boisterously over a few games of pool. At the bar are three guys, one of whom is extremely intoxicated, referring to the bartender as "the original Mexican" and insisting to his fellow patrons that he "needs to make a plan." What he intends to plan for is never revealed before he stumbles out the door.

Another of the trio gets up to leave, bidding a black man named Bill adieu as he wanders away. These three have all known each other for quite awhile, and each live within walking distance. Bill, like the arcade collector, is 58, but isn't as enthusiastic about retiring. He's a Boeing machinist—on strike at the time—and is concerned that he won't be able to afford to stay in the area to be near his grown daughters, who live in South King County, once he retires.

Bill has been in the neighborhood long enough to see it change from a virtually all-black area to one that is now home to Asian supermarkets and pockets of gentrification. He says he doesn't feel comfortable mingling with the yuppies in Columbia City unless he's at Angie's, a rough-and-tumble bar that once represented the neighborhood's status quo but now sticks out like a sore thumb amidst the sleek cafes and 4X4 baby strollers.

Dive Bar Rating:

The Beachcomber

12623 Renton Ave. S.
Phone: 206-772-5183

I first visited Western Europe at the age of 25, three to ten years later than many of my peers. Upon hearing the recaps of their trips, they always sounded a little too Spring Break-y for what I felt should have been an experience that was equal parts intoxication, equal parts cultural indoctrination. Waiting a few years, I reasoned, would give me the maturity to achieve a higher-minded consciousness once I went, and wouldn't put me in debt to boot.

For the most part, I was right. Sure, my friends and I occasionally got hammered, but it was a slower, more vino-centric soiling than it would have been at 22. But Amsterdam really tested our mettle, and not due to its legalized grab bag of narcotica. I was at a bar one afternoon with a friend when we encountered a similarly-aged tourist from the Middle East. My friend had a cursory knowledge of French, while I had a cursory understanding of Spanish and Italian. These cursory understandings got us nowhere with our new friend, and yet we somehow communicated through gesturing and what I can only describe as telepathy (helped along, perhaps, by the hash). Occasional grunts came out of our mouths, if only to prove to one another that we weren't deaf-mutes, but verbal communication proved entirely inessential.

Nine years passed before I experienced a case of déjà vu in regards to that Amsterdam afternoon. This happened in the unlikeliest of places: the Beachcomber in Skyway, an ethnically diverse, staunchly middle class, largely unincorporated neighborhood which occasionally intertwines with the city's southeastern boundaries. While the Beachcomber isn't actually on the beach (it's up the hill), it has a gorgeous neon blue sign befitting of a Hermosa Beach dune dive.It used to be owned by the proprietors of Mike's Chili Parlor, the Semandiris family, whose longtime residential headquarters actually sit on the lakefront below. Hence, the bar's kitchen is held to a higher culinary standard than most, and its delicious, gigantic, homemade jo-jo's are more suited for dinosaurs than humans.

But back to Amsterdam: On the afternoon before Thanksgiving, at approximately 1:30, the bar began filling up with regulars, not one of whom had to tell the bartender what they wanted to drink. She knew exactly what each of them preferred as soon as they walked in the door—'tender-tippler telepathy, if you will. If you want to know what keeps great neighborhood bars afloat, then, it's as simple as communicating with a foreigner with whom you share no linguistic common ground.

Dive Bar Rating: 🍺🍺🍺

Vince's Cocktail Lounge

8824 Renton Ave. S.
Phone: 206-722-2116

In 2002, War Emblem won the Kentucky Derby, and my friend John and I, betting the simulcast at Emerald Downs, won big on that horse. We'd been canny enough to take the Pony Express (Metro's Seattle-Auburn weekender) to the track. If we lost big, we'd take the bus back home. But since we won big, we summoned a cab and decided to embark upon a 30-mile chauffeured pub crawl back to our neck of the woods, which at the time was Queen Anne.

After popping in and out of a couple bars outside the city, we happened upon an Italian pizzeria in the Rainier Valley named Vince's, which happened to have a cocktail lounge. It was late afternoon, and we were the only white people in a dark, smoky bar. Rhythm and blues music blared from the jukebox as a brother who looked like Bo Diddley came up to us and asked us simply, "What are you boys doing?"

He said it nicely, but the unspoken "here" at the end of that question was duly noted. We simply replied that we were having a few drinks, an answer that satisfied him insomuch as it basically had to. What he didn't know was we had about a grand in cash lining our wallets after the Derby score, something that, had we been more sober, we might have taken into account before entering an unfamiliar bar in an equally unfamiliar part of town.

The Vince's of today isn't quite as I remember it. The patrons are still predominantly black, and the jukebox is still dominated by R&B. But the bar seems much brighter and cleaner, and the pizza, with its thin crust and golf ball sausages, is delicious. Additionally, they've got Moretti on tap, and the antipasto salad, served with a side of sardines, is mountainous.

If there's any stratification occurring at Vince's these days, it's between young black adults and customers of their parents' generation—a chasm that isn't germane to Seattle (in St. Louis, for instance, older black bar owners oftentimes set their minimum entry age at 25 or even 30 to keep younger folks out). At a table near the door, a group of twenty-somethings dropping an n-bomb every 30 seconds converses over cocktails. At the bar, where the patrons are much older, an n-bomb still means what an n-bomb meant back when it was commonplace for white people to pepper their sentences with such bigotry. The two generations present at Vince's exchange a knowing glimpse or two, but not much more.

Dive Bar Rating: 🍺🍺

Angie's

4915 Rainier Ave. S.
Phone: 206-722-7771

Before Columbia City became Wallingford with a slightly browner median skin color, the once-slapdash neighborhood's linchpins were the Busy Bee mini-mart and Angie's Tavern, a longstanding watering hole that one expatriate of the nation's capital aptly describes as "more D.C. than Seattle." In other words: the music is thumping, the crowd is mostly black, females' garb can be flashy and suggestive, public displays of affection are SOP, pool hustlers hustle, the drinks are cheap, the bouncer is big, and the interior design an afterthought. Simply put, a weekend night at Angie's is a party—combustible in the best and worst senses of the word.

Bud pitchers can be had for the low, low, non-happy hour price of $5.50 at Angie's, and the bartender is a ringer for New York Knickerbocker Nate Robinson, who played his high school ball a couple miles south on Rainier and his college ball at UW. But one thing that's in short supply at Angie's is top-shelf liquor. Check that: Medium-shelf liquor is tough to come by here; they don't even have Jack Daniels. If the top shelf is going to be that low—and we're talking Gentleman Jack and Cuervo low—the drinks had better be stiff and cheap. On this front, Angie's delivers, offering Olde English tallboys to boot.

As Columbia City continues its march toward gentrification, Angie's is bound to come under increased scrutiny. Occasionally, you'll hear the place mentioned as a hotbed of drugs, drunkenness, and violence. Not to say that sort of thing doesn't exist to some extent at Angie's—it does in just about every bar—but when a neighborhood tends to get too full of itself, hyperbole often masquerades as truth. Let's hope cooler heads prevail in Columbia City, and Angie's is embraced as the cultural and commercial forerunner that it is.

Dive Bar Rating:

Jules Maes

5919 Airport Way
Phone: 206-957-7766

In the summer of 1999, *The Stranger* ran a profile of a 111-year-old Georgetown dive bar, Jules Maes, which included one of the most unfortunate headlines in the history of culinary journalism. "The Bar That Won't Go Away" was the title of the piece. Shortly thereafter, Jules Maes closed.

Fortunately, the closure would prove to be short-lived, as Jules Maes has since been re-opened, with significant enhancements to both its menu and live music calendar. It's a good thing this place has been around for over a century, because otherwise any bar that serves a (very good) marionberry salad would be automatically stripped of its dive status.

Jules Maes is a marvelously well-preserved slice of frontier saloon authenticity. Situated across the street from the original Rainier brewery, the bar's walls boast a host of vintage paraphernalia from that as well as the Olympia brewery that once operated an hour south of town. And there's nothing plastic about the décor, which is all exposed beams and polished wood.

This is not a place to scratch your frou-frou drink itch; one of the bartender's favorite setups is a shot of Hornitos and pickle juice with an Oly back (Smarty Pants down the street serves a bacon martini, it's worth noting). On a Thursday in winter, a 32-year-old gal who also works at the Cha Cha is minding the taps, and remarks that Georgetown is ideal for people who've outgrown Capitol Hill. I've heard many descriptions of Georgetown since it first bloomed into hipsterhood a few years ago, but I've never heard anyone nail it like that.

Dive Bar Rating:

WEST SEATTLE

ALKI
ADMIRAL
THE JUNCTION
WHITE CENTER

Corner Pocket

4302 SW Alaska St.
Phone: 206-933-0320

The Corner Pocket lies beneath Easy Street Records' flagship store, a retailer so wildly popular at West Seattle's hippest corner that they were able to later add a wildly popular diner, where many a hungover hipster takes his hashbrowns with Pabst instead of coffee on a Sunday morn. The entrance to the Corner Pocket actually splits the sister enterprises, insofar that the staircase that leads to the pool hall's subterranean entryway creates a temporary indentation in Easy Street's window scheme.

At the onset of the staircase is the Corner Pocket logo, a retro green rendering featuring a pair of pool sticks and a cocktail glass. The staircase goes deeper and deeper, to where you feel as though you're nearing the bowels of Hell. The paint is chipped, it smells a little, and there's a trail of cigarette butts that leads to the door. Upon cracking the door, you expect to walk into an austere pool room, with cement floors and old metal lockers, whose liquor cabinet begins and ends with Schlitz and Wild Turkey, and whose patrons are ex-cons paroled to minimum wage jobs who need to hustle some off-the-books money to make rent.

Instead what you walk into is a meticulously-maintained, almost arty pool hall, with oil paintings on the wall and a comprehensive selection of top-shelf elixirs. Instead of a beat-up jukebox containing only old Delta blues, the Corner Pocket features an Internet jukebox, which unfortunately has been known to play a little too much rap-rock at the behest of its younger patrons. And instead of a dank back room for high-stakes poker and knuckle sandwiches resulting from delinquent bet payouts, there's a comfortable back area for groups interested in watching sports on a gigantic TV.

Suffice it to say, the Corner Pocket's entryway alone is what classifies it as a dive. But doesn't the imagination's exaggerated buildup count for something?

Dive Bar Rating: 🍺🍺

White Center Eagles Club

10452 15th Ave. SW
Phone: 206-248-1765

Contrary to popular opinion, there are actually white people in White Center, and many of them—especially AARP members—congregate nightly at the White Center Eagles Club. Because of this, karaoke starts a little earlier—7:30 to be exact. But there are few things cooler in life than drinking with people who could pass for your grandparents.

The building that houses the White Center Eagles is set way back from the street, with a large parking lot out front. From the exterior, it looks like a gigantic work shed that should be sitting on a farm, or an old post office. Inside, it looks like a huge, small-town, country and western bar, with an entire rail devoted to pull tabs and $1.50 Budweiser pounders (blue-collarese for "pints"). The jukebox, fittingly, is all country, all the time.

Before karaoke started one night, the club president took the microphone to announce the club's Eagle of the Month. Up strode a lanky, fifty-something guy with an old baseball jacket on. It struck me at this moment that Eagles Clubs and organizations like them are places where people who might go unnoticed in the outside world can feel special and appreciated. It also struck me that this might be the same emotional pull that many a well-worn bar has on people of this ilk. Then it finally struck me that what kept striking me was a lot like the plot (and theme song) from Cheers, at which point I smiled at the bartender, took my last swig of beer, and left.

Dive Bar Rating:

The Locker Room

One magical night at the Locker Room, when the bartender ran out of proper glasses to pour draft beer in, she decided to charge me "half-price." That's right: a mere 65 cents for a pint of Busch, which she shrewdly rounded up from 62.5 (capitalism, baby). I felt like I was drinking during the Depression with an aristocrat's wallet, so I drank a lot. When I called back to confirm that this hadn't, in fact, been a dream (one I dream frequently), I asked the employee who picked up the phone if hers was the place that served the super-cheap Busch. "No, not really," she replied. "So what's the price?" I inquired. "A dollar twenty-five," she said. I then asked what it would cost to rent the utility closet, so I would never have to leave.

A gloriously divey watering hole on White Center's main drag, the Locker Room is full of colorful drinkers from 6 a.m. to close, with no real lull in the action. In White Center, this can be a curse as well as a blessing. While the neighborhood has gotten considerably safer in the last couple decades, actually becoming a destination for bold diners in search of delicious ethnic food (especially Mexican and Vietnamese), it's still looked upon fretfully as a sort of DMZ by most Seattleites. While a small part of White Center rests on the Seattle side of Roxbury Street, its main commercial strip, where the Locker Room sits, is technically in unincorporated King County. The city has tried in recent years to annex the whole of White Center, but has been met with opposition from Burien to the south. The net result is a neighborhood that sits right on the edge of two police department's jurisdictions, creating an ideal atmosphere for drugs, prostitution, and gang violence to flare up, as it still does at times, usually within fairly close proximity of the Locker Room's front entrance.

The daytime regulars don't so much talk at the Locker

Room as they do cackle. The crowd is a fabulously diverse cast of characters, ranging from an old-timer in suspenders playing solitaire at a table by himself, to an antsy younger couple guzzling mixed whiskey drinks who feel as though they have to plot their escape from the bar. There's also a mustachioed alpha male who gets real grabby and loud with the women who stroll in, an elderly couple who appear to be spending their life savings on pull tabs and Milwaukee's Best, and a gaunt, silent, bearded man drinking those cheap glasses of Busch by himself at the corner of the bar. These people all know each other, and know that at the Locker Room, they're not going to be judged.

Dive Bar Rating: 🍺🍺🍺🍺🍺

Magic Lanes

10612 15th Ave. SW
Phone: 206-244-5060

Bowling is the most popular indoor participatory sport in America, and has been for some time. But the bowling landscape has, quite literally, changed dramatically over the last quarter-century. In cities like Seattle, as real estate has increased in value, more and more bowling alley owners have sold out to developers hell bent on maximizing a given parcel's value per square foot. And while boutique nightclub-bowling alley hybrids like Lucky Strike Lanes have managed to carve out a niche, traditional centers are an endangered species.

In Seattle proper, but two remain: West Seattle Bowl and Imperial Lanes. But in White Center, just beyond the city limit, there are two more: Roxbury and Magic Lanes. Most people, however, don't come to these centers to bowl—they come to play cards, as gambling regulations outside of Seattle are far more lax than they are within.

The Magic Lanes bar is a scene unto itself, cut off physically from the bowling area and the gambling parlor, but not the snack bar, with which it shares space. This dynamic means it's not uncommon for a serious juicer to be but a slight partition away from an 11-year-old who just wants to order a box of Dots. While out in the alley, the stereo blares—and I mean *blares*—bass-heavy R&B, the soundtrack in the lounge tends toward adult contemporary. But because the bass in the alley is so thick, if you're sitting in the bar, the aural effect is like a Ludacris-Jewel mash-up, which is pretty bizarre.

Even with the emergence of video game and boutique bowling, the throwback venues still attract a handful of young adults. At Magic Lanes, a trio cute twenty-somethings alternate between bowling, gossipy smoke breaks, and the bar, where one of them orders three Long Island Iced Teas.

The bartender asks if she needs a tray to carry them out to the alley. She demurs, and corrals the cocktails with her bare hands. She's obviously done this before, perhaps even for a living.

Dive Bar Rating:

SPORTIN' DIVES

ROCKSPORT

GOLDIE'S

THE DUCHESS

SLUGGERS

MADISON PUB

THE ADMIRAL PUB

THE CROSSWALK

Marv's Broiler

9808 16th Ave. SW
Phone: 206-763-1412

Marv's Broiler looks like it should be a '50s-style drive-in, with parking stalls and angular beams galore in the parking lot. Short of that, its name suggests that it should be a '60s-style broiler, the sort of place where blue-hairs and families sit down to have a warm, hardy meal. Today, Marv's menu begins and ends with artery-hardening delicacies, the "Broiler" in its name a total cock tease. There is no curbside service. But Marv's has not been shuddered, it has simply been streamlined. Now, it serves mainly as a neighborhood dive bar for Caucasians whose lives after dark exist in the unincorporated no-man's land between Burien and South Roxbury Street. These folks, age 45 and up, have seen the area go from lower middle class white to multi-colored DMZ to multi-colored middle class neighborhood. It's not clear how all they feel about the changes, but Marv's is still very much their clubhouse.

Marv's has a $7 kitchen sink platter of fried appetizers—including gizzards, onion rings, nachos, quesadillas, and chicken strips—that tastes better than expected and can easily serve as dinner for two. Its cocktails are reliably strong. Out back, on the smoking porch, a Richard Petty-looking dude in a black cowboy hat sips from a humungous strawberry daiquiri. Something's not quite right with the image of Richard Petty drinking a strawberry daiquiri. Richard Petty should drink lighter fluid and lighter fluid only.

The crowd at Marv's, as previously indicated, consists of mostly white people who've roamed the neighborhood streets for a long, long time. The tables are filled with mostly old male bullshitters, whose universally hoarse vocal quality makes it sound as though they have cigarettes lodged in their throats. Near the bar, there are two middle-aged guys and a rough-looking woman. They're all completely hammered, and seem on the brink of some sort of massive public domestic quarrel—all three of 'em. But then, in the next moment, they seem ready for a group hug. This intermittent pattern continues for a couple hours, before they announce they're going home to barbecue steaks.

A few minutes later, I spot the trio while waiting for some unnecessary but delicious *tortas* at a taco truck out back of Marv's. They're in a humungous truck, motor running in the parking lot of a flea market across the street. In the parking lot are a couple young Latino guys. The truck peels out, intentionally kicking up dust into the young men's faces before speeding off. You've come a long way, White Center, but you've still got a ways to go.

Dive Bar Rating: 🍺🍺🍺🍺

Mac's Triangle

9454 Delridge Wy. SW
Phone: 206-763-0714

Ever been on a street named Roxbury that doesn't have something of a dubious reputation? Me neither. If Chris Rock is looking for a sequel to his hilarious, politically incorrect skewering of Martin Luther King Jr. Ways the nation wide, Roxbury is where he should turn next.

Mac's Triangle sits at the three-way intersection of Roxbury, Delridge, and 16th Ave. SW, three of Seattle's most foreboding stretches of road. In exterior and nomenclature, Mac's looks like a gay dive bar. The reality is far different; Mac's is a bar that's every bit as tough as the intersection requires, yet every bit as canny as a neighborhood trying to pick itself up by its bootstraps demands.

The bar is owned by a barrel-chested, mustachioed gentleman named Mac. He doubles as bartender, triples as cook, and wears a black T-shirt with his pub's logo on the front and "Livin' the Dream in White Center" on the back. Given that the operation is a one-man show, Mac could be forgiven if he half-assed the sandwiches on his menu. Instead he does the opposite, touting his food as "the best in White Center." On at least one count—a sensational Philly cheese steak—he delivers on this promise.

The crowd that populates Mac's Triangle seems a genial lot of shaggy-haired regulars. Based on the preponderance of conversation, and on the promotions hung on the wall, their main interests include motorcycles, darts, and the Seahawks, not necessarily in that order. Mac's also boasts live music from time to time, a surprisingly extensive selection of microbrews and imports, and a level of cleanliness that belies its drab exterior and geographic notoriety.

About a mile north of Mac's, in Highland Park, is an establishment called Zippy's Giant Burgers, which has sustained lines out the door since it opened last summer. Zippy's

burgers are very big (estimated at 1/3-lb.) and very good. But Mac's serves succulent half-pound patties that are more deserving of the "Giant" moniker than Zippy's. I ordered a double bacon cheeseburger—that's a full pound of beef, for those of you who didn't graduate elementary school—one night that turned out to be the second biggest burger I'd ever attempted to eat in my life. The biggest came at a place called Grandpa Mischeaux's in St. Louis, which served patties as big as a Rottweiler's skull. How they cooked that sucker through, I'll never know.

Dive Bar Rating: 🍺🍺

GOOD FOOD

MIKE'S CHILI PARLOR
THE SLOOP
PACIFIC INN
THE CABIN
ED'S KORT HAUS
MAC'S TRIANGLE
WEDGWOOD BROILER
THE MECCA
JULES MAES

The Barrel

One of the most memorable drinking experiences I've ever had was when a friend and I visited a bar called Lee's Unleaded Blues on Chicago's South Side. Lee's is located on South Chicago Avenue, a foreboding stretch of asphalt where about the only signs of life at night other than Lee's are a handful of package stores. The cab driver who picked us up on the other end of town asked us if we were sure we wanted to go where we said we wanted to go.

We got to Lee's early, sat down at the bar, and ordered straight bourbon. Soon, Lee's began filling up with dapper, middle-aged black folks, and a blues band began to play. After a couple songs, a new singer got up from the audience and strode to the stage. After a couple more songs, a new drummer got up from the audience and strode to the stage. Pretty soon, it became evident that not only were about the only white people in the bar, we were about the only non-musicians in the bar, too. Around midnight, we were fed a free platter of chicken gizzards. The Lee's experience was an all-night, all-star blues jam of the highest caliber; we parted ways smiling and stumbling out the door.

If Seattle has an equivalent to Lee's, it's The Barrel in Top Hat, a peculiarly-named neighborhood between White Center and Burien whose main drag is 1st Ave. S. But unlike Lee's, at the Barrel, the customers are mostly white. On Tuesdays, they have an all-night, all-star blues-rock jam that starts at happy hour and ends at closing time. Longtime local rocker Lynn Sorensen often plays talent curator as well as guitar.

The Barrel's interior is a wide room with picnic tables built for communal drinking. It has drive-in style parking stalls surrounding the structure, and its name emblazoned upon, well, a barrel-like feat of masonry that shoots up from the roof. (It must have been an A&W in a previous life.) The crowd is mainly gritty, working-class white people who don't fuck around when it comes to drinking, and the waitresses are a seasoned collection of brassy, don't-take-shit-from-nobody starlets who won't hesitate to cut you off if you get out of line. But you have to get way o ut of line to invite such a heavy hand at a place like the Barrel, where Friday comes three nights earlier than scheduled.

Dive Bar Rating:

Admiral Pub

2310 California Ave. SW
Phone: 206-933-9500

There's a great big city beyond the shores of Alki to experience, but don't tell that to the staff and regulars at the Admiral Pub, a sprawling neighborhood sports bar that serves as a constant reminder that, in some instances, who happens to live in West Seattle stays in West Seattle.

While watching baseball on one of the Admiral's many TVs, a group of twenty-something dudes were pounding beers and making use of the word "fucking" in adjectival form every fourth word or so as they discussed the success, or lack thereof, of picking up chicks at nearby southwestern-themed hot spots Mission and Matador, both of which are located along California Avenue, the west side's epicenter of everything. At the bar, a couple talked about the prior weekend on Alki Beach, which is as close as Seattle gets to a Southern California cruising scene. The male member of this duo remarked that he might like to catch a screening of *Forgetting Sarah Marshall* across the street at the Admiral Twin, a second-run movie theater. Only in small towns do people wait for movies to arrive at the only movie theater around, and West Seattle, for some people, is a small town; even if, in reality, it's a small city, with a population of around 80,000 people.

Poker night at the Admiral comes every Tuesday. But while the back tables are packed, very few players get up to order drinks—which sort of defeats the purpose of the whole endeavor, at least from the employees' perspective. Behind the bar, a male bartender convinces a female cocktail waitress to prank call one of his friends and sing the phrase "brown chick-a brown cow" into the phone like a funk singer. When a young laborer who's just finished his shift comes up and orders a shot of Jagermeister, the waitress informs him that they're almost out of Jager as she pours him a shot out of a machine that keeps that elixir as well as Tuaca cool behind the bar.

While we're on the topic, the evolution—or devolution, depending on one's personal theory of evolution—of Tuaca from obscure Italian dessert liqueur to shoot it and boot it status has got to be one of the all-time great marketing feats. Can boilermakers please make a comeback already?

Dive Bar Rating: 🍺🍺🍺

Rocksport

4209 SW Alaska St.
Phone: 206-935-5838

What's in a name? At Rocksport, everything. First, "rock": classic rock bands grace the stage of the cavernous Alaska Junction bar several nights a week. (When Hell's Belles, an all-female AC/DC cover band, is the featured act, the place goes buck wild.) Next, "sport": This is a sports bar, and it's built for speed. There are televisions of all sizes affixed to virtually every hard surface in the place, there is random beer and sports paraphernalia everywhere, there's a plethora of fried appetizers on the menu, and well liquor typically does the clientele just fine.

"Just give me my game" should be the bar's mantra. That's all any real sports fan wants, and there aren't nearly enough like-minded establishments within the Seattle city limits that observes this as faithfully as Rocksport does. One thing the bar doesn't deliver is ambiance: It is gray, dark, cavernous, and sort of looks like a Halloween costume superstore, hardly the type of place you'd want to spend drinking away a sunny day.

But remember, rabid sports fans couldn't care less what their surroundings are. They've got tunnel vision, and simply want the option to drown in their sorrows or elation, alcohol being an infinitely versatile emotional companion. If a die-hard Husky or Seahawks follower is intent on watching a road game on a TV somewhere with like-minded fanatics, it could be 85 degrees out with a bathtub full of free beer and Scarlett Johansson laying naked on a shays lounge in his back yard, and he'd still get in his truck and drive to Rocksport, fingers crossed that she'll still be there after the second overtime.

Dive Bar Rating:

Poggie Tavern

4717 California Ave. SW
Phone: 206-937-2165

When you walk into a tavern whose bartender is wearing an Olde English baseball cap, this tends to be a surefire sign that there isn't an ounce of anal retentiveness in the room. Three-and-a-half years on from the smoking ban, the Poggie Tavern still smells like an ashtray, which makes it stick out like a sore thumb on the strip of California Avenue that passes through the hip, well-behaved Alaska Junction. That and the live heavy metal acts, whose ear-rattling sounds explode through the Poggie's rear entrance on weekend nights.

Around happy hour, the Poggie mostly caters to hard laborers who've just punched out for the night. But diversity occasionally comes in the form of a young father of two sneaking in 16 ounces (or more) of relaxation before he must contend with the rug rats at home. Providing childcare while drunk is doubtless a bad idea, but I'm not convinced doing it after a couple nerve-calming pints of golden goodness is such a bad idea. In fact, I'm pretty sure that's how my Dad used to do it, and look at me now.

If ever there were a place you could call a pull-tab bar, the Poggie's it. While live music, darts, and sports on TV serve as useful diversions, the chief source of recreation here—besides, of course, drinking beer—is ripping little tickets. That Washington State is perfectly cool with this potentially addictive and expensive form of alcoholic entertainment yet won't allow booze in strip joints—and really doesn't want to allow strip joints, period—is beyond me. Compared to the laissez faire adult vice policies of Vancouver, B.C. to the north and Portland, Ore. to the south, Seattle might as well be Salt Lake City. Doesn't matter what you're talking about, really—drinking rum and Coke is a lot more fun than drinking Cherry Coke. It just is.

Dive Bar Rating: 🍺🍺🍺🍺

Tug Inn

Aside from having a great moniker that nostalgically winks at Seattle's maritime heritage, the Tug has a clientele that remains largely a mirror of the South Delridge neighborhood it calls home. On a Friday night, shortly after 11, a dozen or so patrons shoot pool, needle one another playfully, and quaff cold, cheap beer in a manner largely foreign to hipper, cocktail-centric haunts in more northerly reaches of town.

With a sound system unshackled from the strictures of head-bobbing deejays, the Tug's customers choose chestnuts by Stevie Ray Vaughan, Van Halen, and Journey on the tavern's classic rock-heavy jukebox. But when someone selects "Smooth Operator" by Sade, a slightly rumpled guy at the bar contorts his body into a slinky groove with the smooth-jazz beat. Before, he'd been playing air organ to Boston's "Long Time," and when a live version of Phil Collins' "In the Air Tonight" comes on, he holds his hand overhead, tapping a pair of imaginary drumsticks in time with the music before launching into an air-drum solo. Simultaneously, at a table in the middle of the room, a husky, drunken, Native American woman with bleach blonde hair is holding court—loudly—before a table full of working folks whose happy hours tend to last all night.

The Tug's main alcoholic attraction is its $3.50 personal pitchers of Pabst, which breaks out to $1.75 a pint. Occasionally, they'll have hot dogs available for purchase; occasionally they won't. It sort of depends on inventory and the bartender's mood, as there's never more than one person on shift at this cozy, ramshackle joint. The Tug's carpet must be a quarter-century old, which is but one of the things that contribute to its "buddy's garage with a couch, TV, and cooler in it" vibe. During last year's NBA conference finals, a couple regulars were assembling a large, steel heating lamp for the patio in between swigs of beer; the place just seems to be in a constant state of refurbishment. It's also the only drinking establishment within stumbling distance of my tiny house on the hill, so I tend to overlook such minor inconveniences.

Dive Bar Rating: 🍺🍺🍺🍺

Redline Music & Sports Bar

4439 35th Ave. SW
Phone: 206-938-3598

The boxcar-like building that houses the Redline has gone through a handful of booze-oriented incarnations in its time, none of them good. Whatever bar's been where the Redline is has been an easy scratch from any West Seattlites' list of places to drink. The place just couldn't seem to shake its bad vibe—until it became the Redline.

Granted, there are still dudes who look like Edward James Olmos prowling around the bar, not to mention some middle-aged bachelors who seem a little too meaty for anyone's good. But owner Scott Goerig has been largely successful in improving his bar's aura with a truly novel approach: he's turned it into Washington State University's best college bar. Never mind that Wazzu is located hundreds of miles east near the Idaho state line. That Goerig, who dresses even his dog in Cougar crimson, has chosen to open his bar in prime Husky habitat makes his success all the more impressive.

The best college bars are like never-ending theme parties. At the Redline, Goerig changes the theme from live music to toga parties to movie and poker nights, but makes sure there's a fresh wrinkle for every night of the week, even if it's just a featured cocktail or something. The bar also offers personalized mugs that guarantee regulars discounted beer. Ultimately, it's about as unpretentious a bar as can be found in Seattle, and it makes for one hell of a Cougar den on game day.

Dive Bar Rating: 🍺🍺🍺

Ebb Tide Room

If beer is for breakfast, then vodka's what's for brunch at the Ebb Tide Room, the adjoining lounge that belongs to the 70-year-old Chelan Café, a family-owned greasy spoon located where the heavy industry of Harbor Island begins to morph into the sands of Alki. There's also a barber shop included in the same building, in case your hair gets too drunk to drive.

An out-of-control car crashed through the Ebb Tide's front wall last year, which allowed the owners to expand the front of the dark, reddish lounge a bit—although the extra square footage serves as little more than a foyer. Whereas pouring country gravy over as many breakfast dishes as possible seems to be the key to the diner's success, obscuring any hint of tonic with a tumbler full of straight vodka seems to work for the bar, as my friend's wife found out on a Saturday morn, when a handful of us decided we needed a little liquid courage before a noontime walk along the trails of nearby Longfellow Creek.

For those who think the notion that people drink before work is a myth, the Ebb Tide's early evening crowd will dispel it. Harbor Island is a bastion of heavy industry where production never shuts down. This means union jobs and graveyard shifts—and guys who've grown tired of their union jobs and graveyard shifts trying to liven them up a little with a pre-grind nip. But while this sort may be the most reliable of the Ebb Tide's denizens, there are few bars in Seattle where the crowd's composition is more unpredictable. One day, it might be several tables full of boisterous couples, reenacting their own blue-collar version of *The Big Chill*. Another day, it might be a large crew of big black dudes who look like they could be on the Seahawks' taxi squad. Other days, it's straight-up, salt-of-the-earth lushes. You just never know what you're going to get at the Ebb Tide, which is a big part of its appeal.

Dive Bar Rating:

Alki Tavern

1321 Harbor Ave.
Phone: 206-932-9970

Seattle's more of a Vespa and bicycle town than a hog town, but that's not to say it doesn't boast a couple great biker bars. Atop the list is West Seattle's Alki Tavern, whose across-the-street neighbor is Puget Sound and which boasts an unobstructed view of the downtown Seattle skyline. That this place, with its cracked blue paint and ramshackle exterior, has been spared the developer's wrecking ball is a minor miracle. But then, if such a perilous plight were in the offing, the passion to salvage the Alki would likely be on par with that devoted to the Blue Moon in past years. The oceanfront tavern is that iconic.

As biker bars go, the Alki is about as easygoing as they come. One afternoon, I witnessed a couple arguing over which kind of pitcher they should order. She wanted something light, he wanted muscle. Seated at the bar was the long, lost third guitarist from ZZ Top—shades, bandana, leather vest…the works. Behind the bar was a muscular 'tender. Together, these two brutes came up with a whale of a mediation plan: Since there are four pints to a pitcher, each drinker would get two pints of his or her choice, at pitcher price. Before that day and to this one, I've yet to see a more reasonable offer come out of a situation where the bar would have been fully justified in charging by the pint.

The Alki's blue façade looks like a garage, with a porthole window on the door and multiple American flags and plant boxes. There is no sign signaling that you've arrived at the Alki Tavern. The bar's interior is surprisingly high-ceilinged and spacious, with old, old etchings covering the Alki's thick wooden tables, booths, benches, and bathrooms. In back, there's a short-order window known as the Coral Sea Cafe where $1 burgers or tacos can be had on certain nights.

The best time to visit the Alki is during the summer. At

this time of year, volleyball nets go up on the beach, scuba divers take to the waters, and cruisers and strollers take to the streets and sidewalks. Around the bend from the bulk of this action, the Alki serves as respite. Dogs lounge out front, while people lounge inside, breathing in wafts of salt air and plowing through pitchers like they're ice water while the Allman Brothers warble away on the jukebox. Hard liquor's great and all, but life's a lot simpler and more coherent when all there is to drink is beer.

Dive Bar Rating:

10 Best Dive Bars

1. **The Rimrock.** The *Twilight Zone* for juicers, with a live magician and Seattle's best cover band.

2. **The Blue Moon.** More famous writers, artists, and drunks have graced the bar of this counterculture icon than any other establishment in the city.

3. **Mike's Chili Parlor.** An enduring paean to Ballard's working-class past, with ice-cold Ouzo and delicious chili that will turn your ass into an active volcano.

4. **The Baranof.** This is the Seafair Pirates' favorite bar, and pirates have been known to drink a little.

5. **The Nite Lite.** Not only downtown's most welcoming dive bar, but downtown's best bar, period.

6. **Moon Temple.** The strongest drinks in town, hands down.

7. **Al's.** At no other place in the city do hipsters and crusty regulars co-exist so harmoniously.

8. **The Sloop.** This is the place to try and match beer-drinking sailors chug-for-chug. Be prepared to lose this match.

9. **Angie's.** A raucous, blackalicious bird-flip to Columbia City gentrification run amok.

10. **The Waterwheel.** Looks like a glorified double-wide where Swayze should be bouncing. But looks are deceiving.

10 Most Intimidating

1. **Kelly's**
2. **Dome Stadium Tavern**
3. **Rose Garden**
4. **Joe's**
5. **The Turf**
6. **Seattle Eagle**
7. **Fortune Sports Bar**
8. **Angie's**
9. **The Locker Room**
10. **Heads or Tails**

Honorable Mention

For reasons mostly having to do with time, budget, redundancy, and the long-term viability of my liver, the following Seattle bars didn't quite crack the Top 100. But they all could have, and are well worth a visit (except maybe for Mel's).

The Sundown (Greenwood)
Bleachers (Greenwood)
Lake City Bar & Grill (Lake City)
The T-Bird (Crown Hill)
Quarter Lounge (First Hill)
West Seattle Eagles (West Seattle)
Mandarin Gate (Oak Tree)
Mel's Tavern (Rainier Valley)

Far-Flung Dives

Following is a criminally incomplete of dives that can be located in the suburbs of Seattle and beyond (in some instances, way beyond):

Doc's Pilchuck Tavern (Machias)
The Doghouse (Everett)
Cloverleaf Tavern (Tacoma)
Magoo's (Tacoma)
Jack's (Auburn)
Tides Tavern (Gig Harbor)
Cozy Inn (Bothell)
Fourth Ave Tavern (Olympia)
The China Clipper (Olympia)
Mt. Si Tavern (North Bend)
Darrel's Tavern (Shoreline)
The Hobnobber (Burien)
Benz Restaurant & Sports Lounge (Boulevard Park)
Trudy's Bar (Seatac)
Sunnydale (Seatac)
Harvey's (Lynnwood)
Liquid Lime (Kirkland)
Palmer's (Redmond)
Chester Club (South Bend)
Yellabeak (Enumclaw)
Whitehorse (Tukwila)
Bubba's Roadhouse (Sultan)
Rolling Log Tavern (Issaquah)
Mike's Tavern (Cle Elum)
Pied Piper (Kent)
Pla Mor Tavern (Maple Valley)
Whistling Post (Skykomish)
The Beaver Inn (Bellingham)
Conway Tavern (Conway)
Toby's Tavern (Coupeville)
Silvana Tavern (Silvana)
Markos (Roslyn)
The Mustard Seed (Bellevue)

Ghosts of Dive Bars Past

Here is an admittedly incomplete list of the ghosts of dive bars past, for whose departures Seattle will forever be worse.

Sorry Charlie's
The Admiral Benbow
Vito's
Uncle Mo's
The County Line
Ileen's/Ernie Steele's
Jade Pagoda
Harvey's (Leary Way)
Chuck & Sally's
The Rendezvous (pre-21st Century facelift)
The Frontier Room (pre-21st Century facelift)
Bogey's
The Lion's Lair (now St. Andrews Pub)
The Doghouse (now the Hurricane)
Gibson's
Vasa Grill (now The People's Pub)
Sunset Tavern (pre-21st Century facelift)
Gay '90s
The Lobo
Kelly's Tavern (now Loretta's, in South Park)
The Mirror
Peking Palace
Deano's
Two Dagos from Texas (now Black Bottle)
The Green Lantern
Buddy's Attic
The Guardsman
The Fremont Triangle (pre-facelift and full booze/food menu)
The Fiddler's Inn (pre-1990s facelift)
The Copper Gate (pre-21st Century facelift)
Happy Palace
Cadillac Jack's
The Soundtrack

And while we'd intended to limit our list to the Seattle city limits, to have done so would have led to the ill-advised exclusion of LaConner's late, great 1890s Inn, eulogized as follows by the novelist and longtime LaConner resident Tom Robbins:

> All during the Seventies, the hottest spot between Seattle and the Canadian border was a funky, joyously rowdy, now legendary tavern in La Conner called the 1890s Inn. The place made a mockery of the word "inn," but it was definitely hospitable, and on Friday and Saturday nights when there was LOUD live music, it was packed elbow to elbow with rock 'n' rollers from a four-county area. (Weekdays, it functioned primarily as a social club for La Conner's painters, poets and bohemians.)
>
> The wooden, false-fronted building, which actually was built in the 1890s, sits atop pilings in the Swinomish Channel, and on dance nights it would shake so hard it threatened to collapse into the water. The atmosphere was freewheeling, almost anarchistic, but Rabbit the bartender (who poured exceedingly generous beers) did have rules, one of which was joints could only be smoked out on the deck. Oddly enough—or maybe not—fisticuffs and arguments were practically unheard of.
>
> Once during Smelt Derby (back before civilization destroyed the smelt runs and the derby was still fun), so many eager patrons were trying to gain entry to the already overcrowded 1890s that the front door was ripped off of its hinges. They don't make beer parlors like that anymore.

Ghosts of Dive Bars Future

In the event that a second edition of this book is commissioned at some point, the following drinking establishments might stand a chance of making it—but only if they let themselves go completely to seed (i.e., bathroom cleaning shall be limited to once a week, and no fresh paint allowed).

Linda's (Capitol Hill)
The Cuff (Capitol Hill)
Mars Bar (Eastlake/Cascade)
Victory Lounge (Eastlake/Cascade)
Re-Bar (Denny Triangle)
Owl & Thistle (Pioneer Square)
The Boxcar Alehouse (Magnolia)
Hooverville (SoDo)
Tin Hat (Ballard/Phinney)
Sully's Snowgoose Saloon (Phinney Ridge)
The Bottleneck Lounge (Madison Valley)
Tigers (Broadview)
Brewsky's (White Center)
The Highliner (Magnolia)
Redwood (Capitol Hill)

Index
(bars arranged alphabetically)